Get Ready!

FOR STANDARDIZED TESTS

D0775306

GRADE FOUR

Other Books in the Get Ready! Series:

Get Ready! for Standardized Tests: Grade 1 by Joseph Harris, Ph.D.

Get Ready! for Standardized Tests: Grade 2 by Joseph Harris, Ph.D.

Get Ready! for Standardized Tests: Grade 3 by Karen Mersky, Ph.D.

Get Ready! for Standardized Tests: Grade 5 by Leslie E. Talbott, Ph.D.

Get Ready! for Standardized Tests: Grade 6 by Shirley Vickery, Ph.D.

Get Ready!

FOR STANDARDIZED TESTS

GRADE FOUR 4

Joseph Harris, Ph.D.

Carol Turkington
Series Editor

McGraw-Hill

New York   San Francisco Washington, D.C. Auckland Bogotá
Caracas Lisbon London Madrid Mexico City Milan
Montreal New Delhi San Juan Singapore
Sydney Tokyo Toronto

Library of Congress Cataloging-in-Publication Data

Get ready! for standardized tests / c Carol Turkington, series editor.
    p. cm.
  Includes bibliographical references.
  Contents: [1] Grade 1 / Joseph Harris — [2] Grade 2 / Joseph Harris — [3] Grade 3 /
Karen Mersky — [4] Grade 4 / Joseph Harris — [5] Grade 5 / Leslie E. Talbott — [6]
Grade 6 / Shirley Vickery.
  ISBN 0-07-136010-7 (v. 1) — ISBN 0-07-136011-5 (v. 2) — ISBN 0-07-136012-3 (v.
3)
  — ISBN 0-07-136013-1 (v. 4) — ISBN 0-07-136014-X (v. 5) — ISBN 0-07-136015-8 (v.
6)
   1. Achievement tests—United States—Study guides. 2. Education, Elementary—United
States—Evaluation. 3. Education, Elementary—Parent participation—United States. I
Turkington, Carol. II. Harris, Joseph.

LB3060.22 .G48 2000

McGraw-Hill

A Division of The McGraw·Hill Companies

1 2 3 4 5 6 7 8 9 0 PBT/PBT 0 9 8 7 6 5 4 3 2 1 0

ISBN 0-07-136013-1

This book was set in New Century Schoolbook by Inkwell Publishing Services.

Printed and bound by Phoenix Book Technology.

McGraw-Hill books are available at special quantity discounts to use as pre-
miums and sales promotions, or for use in corporate training programs. For
more information, please write to the Director of Special Sales, McGraw-
Hill, Professional Publishing, Two Penn Plaza, New York, NY 10121-2298.
Or contact your local bookstore.

To my favorite hopes for our future:
Kara Kennedy
T. J. McNamara
the newest arrival, John William Harris
and last, but never least, my son, Ross Adam Harris

Contents

Chapter 9. Math Applications   59

Appendix A: Web Sites and Resources for More Information   69

Appendix B: Read More about It   73

Appendix C: What Your Child's Test Scores Mean   75

Appendix D: Which States Require Which Tests   83

Appendix E: Testing Accommodations   93

Glossary   95

Answer Keys for Practice Skills   97

Sample Practice Test   99

Answer Key for Sample Practice Test   126

SKILLS CHECKLIST

MY CHILD . . .	HAS LEARNED	IS WORKING ON
VOCABULARY		
Synonyms		
Antonyms		
Multi-meaning words		
Words in context		
Word study		
READING COMPREHENSION		
Critical reading		
Literal comprehension		
Inferential comprehension		
LANGUAGE MECHANICS		
Capitalization		
Punctuation		
Parts of speech		
LANGUAGE EXPRESSION		
Usage		
Sentences		
Paragraphs		
SPELLING AND STUDY SKILLS		
Spelling		
Study skills		
MATH CONCEPTS		
Numeration		
Number concepts		
Number properties		
Fractions and decimals		
MATH COMPUTATION		
Math facts		
Regrouping		
Addition		
Subtraction		
Multiplication		
Division		
MATH APPLICATIONS		
Geometry		
Measurement		
Word problems		

Introduction

Almost all of us have taken standardized tests in school. We spent several days bubbling-in answers, shifting in our seats. No one ever told us why we took the tests or what they would do with the results. We just took them and never heard about them again.

Today many parents aren't aware they are entitled to see their children's permanent records and, at a reasonable cost, to obtain copies of any information not protected by copyright, including testing scores. Late in the school year, most parents receive standardized test results with confusing bar charts and detailed explanations of scores that few people seem to understand.

In response to a series of negative reports on the state of education in this country, Americans have begun to demand that something be done to improve our schools. We have come to expect higher levels of accountability as schools face the competing pressures of rising educational expectations and declining school budgets. High-stakes standardized tests are rapidly becoming the main tool of accountability for students, teachers, and school administrators. If students' test scores don't continually rise, teachers and principals face the potential loss of school funding and, ultimately, their jobs. Summer school and private after-school tutorial program enrollments are swelling with students who have not met score standards or who, everyone agrees, could score higher.

While there is a great deal of controversy about whether it is appropriate for schools to use standardized tests to make major decisions about individual students, it appears likely that standardized tests are here to stay. They will be used to evaluate students, teachers, and the schools; schools are sure to continue to use students' test scores to demonstrate their accountability to the community.

The purposes of this guide are to acquaint you with the types of standardized tests your children may take; to help you understand the test results; and to help you work with your children in skill areas that are measured by standardized tests so they can perform as well as possible.

Types of Standardized Tests

The two major types of group standardized tests are *criterion-referenced tests* and *norm-referenced tests*. Think back to when you learned to tie your shoes. First Mom or Dad showed you how to loosen the laces on your shoe so that you could insert your foot; then they showed you how to tighten the laces—but not too tight. They showed you how to make bows and how to tie a knot. All the steps we just described constitute what is called a *skills hierarchy:* a list of skills from easiest to most difficult that are related to some goal, such as tying a shoelace.

Criterion-referenced tests are designed to determine at what level students are performing on various skills hierarchies. These tests assume that development of skills follows a sequence of steps. For example, if you were teaching shoelace tying, the skills hierarchy might appear this way:

1. Loosen laces.
2. Insert foot.
3. Tighten laces.
4. Make loops with both lace ends.
5. Tie a square knot.

Criterion-referenced tests try to identify how far along the skills hierarchy the student has progressed. There is no comparison against anyone else's score, only against an expected skill level. The main question criterion-referenced tests ask is: "Where is this child in the development of this group of skills?"

Norm-referenced tests, in contrast, are typically constructed to compare children in their abilities as to different skills areas. Although the experts who design test items may be aware of skills hierarchies, they are more concerned with how much of some skill the child has mastered, rather than at what level on the skills hierarchy the child is.

Ideally, the questions on these tests range from very easy items to those that are impossibly difficult. The essential feature of norm-referenced tests is that scores on these measures can be compared to scores of children in similar groups. They answer this question: "How does the child compare with other children of the same age or grade placement in the development of this skill?"

This book provides strategies for increasing your child's scores on both standardized norm-referenced and criterion-referenced tests.

The Major Standardized Tests

Many criterion-referenced tests currently in use are created locally or (at best) on a state level,

and there are far too many of them to go into detail here about specific tests. However, children prepare for them in basically the same way they do for norm-referenced tests.

A very small pool of norm-referenced tests is used throughout the country, consisting primarily of the Big Five:

- California Achievement Tests (CTB/McGraw-Hill)
- Iowa Tests of Basic Skills (Riverside)
- Metropolitan Achievement Test (Harcourt-Brace & Company)
- Stanford Achievement Test (Psychological Corporation)
- TerraNova [formerly Comprehensive Test of Basic Skills] (McGraw-Hill)

These tests use various terms for the academic skills areas they assess, but they generally test several types of reading, language, and mathematics skills, along with social studies and science. They may include additional assessments, such as of study and reference skills.

How States Use Standardized Tests

Despite widespread belief and practice to the contrary, group standardized tests are designed to assess and compare the achievement of groups. They are *not* designed to provide detailed diagnostic assessments of individual students. (For detailed individual assessments, children should be given individual diagnostic tests by properly qualified professionals, including trained guidance counselors, speech and language therapists, and school psychologists.) Here are examples of the types of questions group standardized tests are designed to answer:

- How did the reading achievement of students at Valley Elementary School this year compare with their reading achievement last year?

- How did math scores at Wonderland Middle School compare with those of students at Parkside Middle School this year?

- As a group, how did Hilltop High School students compare with the national averages in the achievement areas tested?

- How did the district's first graders' math scores compare with the district's fifth graders' math scores?

The fact that these tests are designed primarily to test and compare groups doesn't mean that test data on individual students isn't useful. It does mean that when we use these tests to diagnose individual students, we are using them for a purpose for which they were not designed.

Think of group standardized tests as being similar to health fairs at the local mall. Rather than check into your local hospital and spend thousands of dollars on full, individual tests for a wide range of conditions, you can go from station to station and take part in different health screenings. Of course, one would never diagnose heart disease or cancer on the basis of the screening done at the mall. At most, suspicious results on the screening would suggest that you need to visit a doctor for a more complete examination.

In the same way, group standardized tests provide a way of screening the achievement of many students quickly. Although you shouldn't diagnose learning problems solely based on the results of these tests, the results can tell you that you should think about referring a child for a more definitive, individual assessment.

An individual student's group test data should be considered only a point of information. Teachers and school administrators may use standardized test results to support or question hypotheses they have made about students; but these scores must be used alongside other information, such as teacher comments, daily work, homework, class test grades, parent observations, medical needs, and social history.

Valid Uses of Standardized Test Scores

Here are examples of appropriate uses of test scores for individual students:

- Mr. Cone thinks that Samantha, a third grader, is struggling in math. He reviews her file and finds that her first- and second-grade standardized test math scores were very low. Her first- and second-grade teachers recall episodes in which Samantha cried because she couldn't understand certain math concepts, and mention that she was teased by other children, who called her "Dummy." Mr. Cone decides to refer Samantha to the school assistance team to determine whether she should be referred for individual testing for a learning disability related to math.

- The local college wants to set up a tutoring program for elementary school children who are struggling academically. In deciding which youngsters to nominate for the program, the teachers consider the students' averages in different subjects, the degree to which students seem to be struggling, parents' reports, and standardized test scores.

- For the second year in a row, Gene has performed poorly on the latest round of standardized tests. His teachers all agree that Gene seems to have some serious learning problems. They had hoped that Gene was immature for his class and that he would do better this year; but his dismal grades continue. Gene is referred to the school assistance team to determine whether he should be sent to the school psychologist for assessment of a possible learning handicap.

Inappropriate Use of Standardized Test Scores

Here are examples of how schools have sometimes used standardized test results inappropriately:

- Mr. Johnson groups his students into reading groups solely on the basis of their standardized test scores.

- Ms. Henry recommends that Susie be held back a year because she performed poorly on the standardized tests, despite strong grades on daily assignments, homework, and class tests.

- Gerald's teacher refers him for consideration in the district's gifted program, which accepts students using a combination of intelligence test scores, achievement test scores, and teacher recommendations. Gerald's intelligence test scores were very high. Unfortunately, he had a bad cold during the week of the standardized group achievement tests and was taking powerful antihistamines, which made him feel sleepy. As a result, he scored too low on the achievement tests to qualify.

The public has come to demand increasingly high levels of accountability for public schools. We demand that schools test so that we have hard data with which to hold the schools accountable. But too often, politicians and the public place more faith in the test results than is justified. Regardless of whether it's appropriate to do so and regardless of the reasons schools use standardized test results as they do, many schools base crucial programming and eligibility decisions on scores from group standardized tests. It's to your child's advantage, then, to perform as well as possible on these tests.

Two Basic Assumptions

The strategies we present in this book come from two basic assumptions:

1. Most students can raise their standardized test scores.

2. Parents can help their children become stronger in the skills the tests assess.

This book provides the information you need to learn what skill areas the tests measure, what general skills your child is being taught in a particular grade, how to prepare your child to take the tests, and what to do with the results. In the appendices you will find information to help you decipher test interpretations; a listing of which states currently require what tests; and additional resources to help you help your child to do better in school and to prepare for the tests.

A Word about Coaching

This guide is *not* about coaching your child. When we use the term *coaching* in referring to standardized testing, we mean trying to give someone an unfair advantage, either by revealing beforehand what exact items will be on the test or by teaching "tricks" that will supposedly allow a student to take advantage of some detail in how the tests are constructed.

Some people try to coach students in shrewd test-taking strategies that take advantage of how the tests are supposedly constructed rather than strengthening the students' skills in the areas tested. Over the years, for example, many rumors have been floated about "secret formulas" that test companies use.

This type of coaching emphasizes ways to help students obtain scores they didn't earn—to get something for nothing. Stories have appeared in the press about teachers who have coached their students on specific questions, parents who have tried to obtain advance copies of tests, and students who have written down test questions after taking standardized tests and sold them to others. Because of the importance of test security, test companies and states aggressively prosecute those who attempt to violate test security—and they should do so.

How to Raise Test Scores

Factors that are unrelated to how strong students are but that might artificially lower test scores include anything that prevents students from making scores that accurately describe their actual abilities. Some of those factors are:

- giving the tests in uncomfortably cold or hot rooms;

- allowing outside noises to interfere with test taking; and

- reproducing test booklets in such small print or with such faint ink that students can't read the questions.

Such problems require administrative attention from both the test publishers, who must make sure that they obtain their norms for the tests under the same conditions students face when they take the tests; and school administrators, who must ensure that conditions under which their students take the tests are as close as possible to those specified by the test publishers.

Individual students also face problems that can artificially lower their test scores, and parents can do something about many of these problems. Stomach aches, headaches, sleep deprivation, colds and flu, and emotional upsets due to a recent tragedy are problems that might call for the student to take the tests during make-up sessions. Some students have physical conditions such as muscle-control problems, palsies, or difficulty paying attention that require work over many months or even years before students can obtain accurate test scores on standardized tests. And, of course, some students just don't take the testing seriously or may even intentionally perform poorly. Parents can help their children overcome many of these obstacles to obtaining accurate scores.

Finally, with this book parents are able to help their children raise their scores by:

- increasing their familiarity (and their comfort level) with the types of questions on standardized tests;

- drills and practice exercises to increase their skill in handling the kinds of questions they will meet; and

- providing lots of fun ways for parents to help their children work on the skill areas that will be tested.

Test Questions

The favorite type of question for standardized tests is the multiple-choice question. For example:

1. The first President of the United States was:

A Abraham Lincoln

B Martin Luther King, Jr.

C George Washington

D Thomas Jefferson

The main advantage of multiple-choice questions is that it is easy to score them quickly and accurately. They lend themselves to optical scanning test forms, on which students fill in bubbles or squares and the forms are scored by machine. Increasingly, companies are moving from paper-based testing to computer-based testing, using multiple-choice questions.

The main disadvantage of multiple-choice questions is that they restrict test items to those that can be put in that form. Many educators and civil rights advocates have noted that the multiple-choice format only reveals a superficial understanding of the subject. It's not possible with multiple-choice questions to test a student's ability to construct a detailed, logical argument on some issue or to explain a detailed process. Although some of the major tests are beginning to incorporate more subjectively scored items, such as short answer or essay questions, the vast majority of test items continue to be in multiple-choice format.

In the past, some people believed there were special formulas or tricks to help test-takers determine which multiple-choice answer was the correct one. There may have been some truth to *some* claims for past tests. Computer analyses of some past tests revealed certain biases in how tests were constructed. For example, the old advice to pick *D* when in doubt appears to have been valid for some past tests. However, test publishers have become so sophisticated in their ability to detect patterns of bias in the formulation of test questions and answers that they now guard against it aggressively.

In Chapter 1, we provide information about general test-taking considerations, with advice on how parents can help students overcome testing obstacles. The rest of the book provides information to help parents help their children strengthen skills in the tested areas.

Joseph Harris, Ph.D.

Test-Taking Basics

Welcome to fourth grade! As your child nears the end of the elementary school years, he'll begin to take on more personal responsibility than he did last year. By the age of 9 or 10, you'll notice that your child has begun to develop a greater capacity for organized, logical thought. He'll be able to perform multiple classification tasks, move objects in a logical sequence, and begin to think of others beyond himself.

As his thoughts become more abstract, your child can begin to incorporate the principles of formal logic. He can come up with his own abstract propositions, and think about a variety of ideas and their possible outcomes. In addition, as his thinking becomes less tied to concrete reality, he can begin to handle proportions, algebraic manipulation, and other purely abstract processes (for example, if $a + b = x$, then $x = a - b$).

School changes quite dramatically for students in fourth grade. Your child is no longer focusing on learning basic reading skills; now he's applying these skills in a wide variety of subjects, including social studies, science, and health. In mathematics, your child will work on reviewing basic math skills before beginning to learn more sophisticated concepts in the later years of elementary school and the beginning of middle school. Study skills become very important, because students will now be asked to write reports, handle long-term assignments, and complete projects.

Keeping these points in mind, there are some basic strategies that you can use to help your child prepare for standardized tests.

Basic Test-Taking Strategies

Sometimes children score lower than you expect on standardized tests because they don't approach testing with the best possible attitude. The goal in preparing for standardized testing is not to "cheat the system" into thinking your child is more gifted than he actually is, but to make sure the tests accurately reflect his capabilities.

Before the Test

Be Patient. Perhaps the most effective thing you can do when preparing your child for standardized tests is be patient. Remember that no matter how much pressure you put on your child, he won't learn anything until he's mentally and emotionally ready.

That doesn't mean you can't offer suggestions and guidance; but there's a fine line between encouraging your child to try challenging tasks he's ready for, and pushing him to perform beyond his ability. If you see that your child isn't making progress, it may be time to give him a break.

Remember that not every child is alike, nor is every child necessarily a clone of Mom or Dad. There's a huge continuum of ability and no set timetable by which to acquire skills.

Talk with Your Child. The best way to figure out areas of strengths and weakness is simply to *pay attention*. Read papers and homework that come home from school; study newsletters prepared by the teacher. If possible, offer to volunteer in the classroom so you can get an idea of not just what's being taught, but how the other children are learning and developing. You might learn that your child isn't abnormally slow at math at all, when you see his performance in the context of the fourth-grade classroom.

Remember to watch for potential vision and hearing problems during this year. Third through fourth grade is often a time when a child's eyes begin to change; many children in fourth grade begin to wear glasses. If your child already wears glasses, you can expect his vision to change somewhat on a yearly basis during the elementary years. Make sure he visits an eye doctor every year to keep his prescription up to date.

Talk with Your Child's Teacher. It's amazing how many parents contact psychologists to have their children evaluated for learning disabilities or emotional disturbance because of problems they think their child *might* be having in school, when they've never spoken with the teacher about their concerns. Don't wait for an invitation or for problems to develop before you meet your child's teacher. Get to know the teacher as early in the school year as possible.

Talk with your child's teacher right away, at the beginning of the year, before a problem begins. Help your child's teacher see you as an ally, someone she is comfortable talking to, before problems develop. Most teachers are eager to keep you updated on your child's progress, and they can give you materials and suggest activities for helping your child at home.

Don't Change Your Child's Routine. Many guides that schools send home to parents before their children take standardized tests give such mistaken advice as having children go to bed early the night before the test or eating a high-protein breakfast on the morning of the test. Instead, you should change as little as possible in your child's routine the day before and the morning of the test. If your child isn't used to going to bed at 8 p.m., then putting him to bed early the night before the test will only frustrate him and may actually make it more difficult for him to get to sleep by the normal time. If he is used to highly sugared cereal or just some buttered toast for breakfast, eating a huge morning meal will only make him feel uncomfortable or sleepy.

If you'd like to try an earlier bedtime, by all means do so—but not the night before the exam. Make that change weeks before testing. If your child is eating fudge and candy for breakfast, introduce a healthier alternative as far in advance as possible. The most productive steps you can take toward preparing your child for standardized tests include helping him to be a healthier and academically stronger student every day.

Neatness. Yes, neatness counts. Check how neatly your child can fill in the bubbles, squares, and rectangles. Coloring outside the lines may be terrific for creative endeavors, but if your child can't fill in a bubble neatly, he may not do as well on the standardized test scored by a computer that reads extraneous bubble marks as errors.

If you've got a computer, you can easily make your own bubble sheets of capital *O*s, squares, rectangles, and triangles your child can practice filling in. Or have him experiment on the example shown on page 9.

During the Test

Once you've prepared your child to get ready for standardized tests, offer him some tips that he can use during the test to help his performance. You don't need to make your child overanxious by spending two hours drilling him on these strategies the night before the test. Instead, a month or so beforehand, calmly bring some of these issues up and discuss them. You might mention your

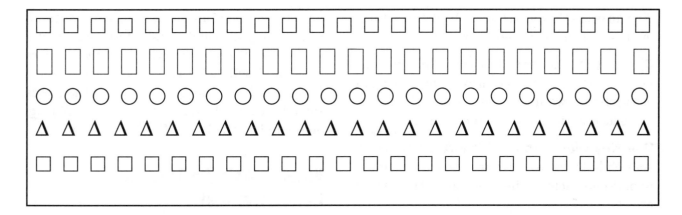

own past standardized test performances.

Then, over the weeks before the test, bring up these strategies in a warm, friendly manner. Talk about the strategies with your child and remind him of them from time to time.

Following these tips has been shown to result in some degree of improvement in test scores.

Bring Extra Pencils. If your child is constantly getting up to sharpen pencils, he's wasting precious time he could be using to answer several more questions. Make sure he has extras so that if the pencil point breaks or gets dull, all he has to do is reach for another. He'll have more time to work on test questions.

Listen Carefully. Children make many mistakes on standardized tests just by not listening to instructions or by not paying attention to demonstrations. Some children put checkmarks inside the bubbles, or they circle the bubbles instead of filling them in. Some forget to put their names on the answer sheets, and still others begin marking their answers on the wrong side of the form or go to the wrong section to begin marking.

Make Sure to Mark the Bubble for the Correct Question. Impress on your child that he mustn't make a mark without being sure that he is marking the correct bubble. If he ends up with some empty bubbles and some with more than one mark, it will be counted against him. Make sure he understands that a computer will be scanning his paper. The more neatly he can fill in the bubbles, the better.

Read the Whole Question First. Make sure your child knows not to dive right into the test, filling in the bubble without thinking about the question. Often the last couple of words in a question give valuable hints about the right answer. There are no extra points for finishing first!

Read All the Answer Choices. Even if your child is *sure* he knows the answer, tell him to carefully read each answer. He might assume the first answer looks good, but the one at the end might be even better.

Skip Difficult Items and Return to Them Later. If your child is a perfectionist, he may well stall at a question he doesn't know and spend too much time worrying about what the correct answer is. Train your child to work through the questions he knows first, and then come back to all the others. Although this strategy won't work with listening tests, it will work with most other types of standardized tests.

A Picture Is Worth a Thousand Words. If there's a picture on the test, teach your child to pay close attention to it. The pictures may give valuable clues that your child can use to help him find the correct answers.

The First Isn't Always the Best. Going with your first knee-jerk response to a question is not always the best idea. Recent research suggests that if you get the urge to change an answer, more likely you *should*. Research has also shown that students can improve scores by flagging answers they aren't sure about and returning to consider them again.

Check the Context. Tell your child that he may find clues to correct answers by looking at descriptions, wording, and other information embedded in the questions themselves.

Use Key Words to Find the Answer. Teach your child to try to determine the parts that are important to solving the question and those that aren't.

Watch for Absolute Words. There aren't many guarantees in life, and apparently not in standardized tests, either. Absolute words such as "never" and "always" are clues that the answer using them is less likely to be correct.

Narrow Down the Choices! If there are four possible answers and you don't have any idea which one is right, you have less chance of guessing correctly than if you're able to narrow down the possibilities to two. If your child is allowed to mark in the test booklets, and he's having trouble deciding which answer is correct, he should first cross out impossible answers; then he can focus on the remaining choices.

Rewrite Math Problems. Your child may find it easy to solve a subtraction problem written in the traditional two-deck format:

$$\begin{array}{r} 25 \\ -\ 19 \\ \hline \end{array}$$

but fall apart when the problem is written in linear fashion: 25 − 19. If that's the case, tell him he can (if allowed) simply rewrite the problem vertically in the margins or other blank space on the test booklet. *Be sure to tell your child to ask if it's acceptable to write in the margins before doing so.*

Tips for You, the Parent

The most important thing to keep in mind about your child's testing is not to be overly anxious about test scores, although you should certainly encourage your child to take tests seriously. If you're up all night worrying the night before, your child will sense your anxiety. Don't make things harder for him. When you get the scores, reread the introduction to this book: Don't judge your child on the basis of a simple test score.

What to Ask the Teacher before the Test

- How will the teacher or the school use the results of the test?
- Which tests will be administered during the school year and for what purposes?
- What other means of evaluation will the teacher or the school use to measure your child's performance?

What to Ask the Teacher after the Test

- How do students in your child's school compare with students in other school systems in your state and across the country?
- What do the test results mean about your child's skills and abilities?
- Are the test results consistent with your child's performance in the classroom?
- What can you do at home to help your child strengthen particular skills?

In the Next Chapter

Now that you've learned how best to prepare before the standardized tests, it's time to move on to learning more about individual skills your child will learn in fourth grade, and what sorts of questions standardized tests will ask to assess how well your child has mastered those skills.

CHAPTER 2

Vocabulary

You probably still remember the very first words your child spoke, those first halting attempts at verbal communication with another human being. The language your child uses is based on what she hears from you, and what your child learns at home about words supports her success in school. In fact, a great deal of the learning that takes place at home is effective because it isn't a repeat of school. When it becomes too formal and too "school-like," it loses its appeal.

What Your Fourth Grader Should Be Learning

By the fourth grade, your child's language should be growing in complexity, so that her vocabulary is beginning to have richness and diversity. A sunset could be pretty, but it could also be beautiful, gorgeous, or incredible.

Your fourth grader should understand that words have opposites and similarities and multiple meanings, and that the context of a word can be used to help decode its meaning. She should be able to decode many words on standardized tests. She should be able to find words in a dictionary and should be aware that many English words actually came from far older terms in other languages. Fourth graders should feel comfortable picking out common prefixes, suffixes, and roots of English words.

What Tests May Ask

If your child has a good vocabulary and has grown up in a home where reading and language are respected, she shouldn't have a problem with vocabulary on standardized tests. By this age, children can make educated guesses on tests, eliminating answers that are obviously wrong and concentrating on what's left. No matter which standardized test your child might encounter, specific areas that most tests assess include:

- synonyms,
- antonyms,
- multi-meaning words,
- words in context, and
- word study.

What You and Your Child Can Do

The language your child uses is based on what she hears from you. Your job is to create an environment that enriches what a child hears, because the words she hears are those she'll use. Pay attention to the words you say and how you use them. If your child hears you say "I seen it," she'll imitate that language. And most likely, if she speaks that way, she'll write that way.

The best way to strengthen a child's vocabulary skills is to read to her. Set aside a regular time each day to read to your children. Read books on a wide range of subjects and have them select what you read. If Cimmie has an interest in music, read about composers and instrument makers. If Tom loves aliens, read about astronomy and Venus.

Encourage your child to continue to read independently; take regular trips with her to the bookstore and the library, and encourage her to read about a wide variety of subjects. Take your child to places where she can expand her interests, where she not only can find more reading materials but can meet others who share her interests.

Family Discussions. Turn off the TV and talk to each other around the dinner table. That's one of the few times an entire family is together; but these days if you don't set some ground rules, there may not be a lot of communication going on. To start with, try "No eating and running," or "Everyone has to have something to talk about" during and after supper. Talk about things going on in the neighborhood, upcoming vacations, what happened at school, events that are coming up, family plans, family decisions. Remember, the conversation should be pleasant and relaxing. This is *not* the time to bring up that unpleasant scene at breakfast or why the bathroom hasn't been cleaned in two weeks.

Post the Spelling List. Post your child's weekly spelling list on the refrigerator door. Use those words with your child as go about your weekly schedule. Encourage her to use the words, too. Make a joke of it to see how many times you both can use the words.

Word of the Week. This family game can be fun to play around the dinner table. Let your child choose the first word; have her write a word on a card and post it on the refrigerator door. For the next week, everyone must use that word as much as possible. Each succeeding week, take turns with different family members posting different words, until it's back to the first child again. As the words are used, they're posted so no one forgets them.

Twenty Questions. This traditional favorite can be a real boost to learning new vocabulary. One family member thinks of an object and the others must guess what it is by asking no more than 20 questions. The first question is always: "Is it animal, vegetable, or mineral?" This covers virtually every possible thing the child could think of. Then, question by question, the field is narrowed to likely possibilities. After the first question, all other questions must take yes-or-no answers.

The value of this game is that it teaches not just vocabulary, but logic as well. You can show your child how to move from broad-based questions ("Is it located in the southern hemisphere?") to those that are gradually more specific ("Is it in the United States?" "Is it in Pennsylvania?" and so on).

Diary. Buy your child a diary (locked versions are popular with this age group) and let her write her thoughts every day.

Learn New Words. Let your fourth grader see you adding new words to your vocabulary all the time. Put the family dictionary in a prominent place, and use it in front of your child. Encourage your child to do the same thing.

Find a Pen Pal. Writing to a pen pal (especially in another country) can provide lots of wonderful spelling practice—and the chance to learn some vocabulary words in other languages as well. Pen pals are offered by a variety of organizations; international e-mail pals are also a popular choice.

Magazines. Give your child a subscription to her favorite magazine. There are plenty of choices for just about every hobby or interest you can think of. Kids this age love to get mail—any kind of mail—and information from the articles provides ideal subjects for family discussions.

Start a Homonym List. Tack up a sheet of paper on the refrigerator and have the whole family write down homonyms. Homonyms are words that sound alike but are spelled differently and mean something different, as in "one" and "won." Ask everyone to add to the list. You'll be surprised at how many homonyms they'll uncover.

Guessing. Even at this age, you can play guessing games in the car with your child, who will probably find it entertaining.

> I'm thinking of a word that starts with "sl" that is something you do in the winter (sled).
>
> I'm thinking of a word that starts with "sh" that is something we do when we're cold (shiver).

Revolving Blend. In this family game, one person starts a common blend, such as "st," and in sequence around the table or room, everyone must think of a word that begins with that blend (stool, student, stir, stripe, sty, stack, and so on). When the list is exhausted, the last person begins another blend, such as "fl" (fly, flay, flea, flight). This game works well for those long car rides.

Letter Find. This is another good car game, although it can be played anywhere. It takes at least two people. As you ride, one player chooses a letter and then everyone must call out everything they see that begins with the letter. One point is awarded for each word, and each person must add up his or her own list. (This teaches math as well!)

Sign Find. A twist on "letter find" is to search for each letter in the alphabet according to the letters you see on a sign. One child takes one side of the road, and another takes the other side. Both start with the letter A and they must search for that letter until it appears on a sign. Then they move on to B. The first person to reach Z wins.

Vocabulary Software. Educational computer software games can get kids brushing up on their skills without knowing they're doing anything other than having fun. Two good choices

for this age group are *Mayhem—The Vocabulary Game* and *Reading Blaster Vocabulary*. If your child's vocabulary skills are advanced for her age, try *Multimedia Vocabulary*.

Synonyms and Antonyms

You can expect the standardized tests your child will take to include a section of synonyms (words that have the same meanings) and antonyms (words with opposite meanings) presented in multiple-choice format.

By the middle years, your child is beginning to develop enough complexity in her language so that she knows many ways to say the same thing and has the ability to figure out the opposite meanings. Fourth graders should be comfortable with the term "synonym" and will continue to study the concept, learning more and more sophisticated examples. Because they are now experts at understanding abstract and complex terms, they will be able to identify a wide range of synonyms.

Keep in Mind. If your fourth grader has trouble remembering the difference between "synonym" and "antonym," remind her that "synonym" and "same as" both start with "s"; and that "antonym" and "anti" (against or opposite) both begin with "a."

Practice Skill: Synonyms/Antonyms

Directions: Read each item and choose the word that means the same as the underlined word.

1 She was <u>grateful</u> for the gift.

   Ⓐ   appreciative

   Ⓑ   angry

   Ⓒ   needy

   Ⓓ   hungry

2 I think my dog is a <u>female</u>.

   Ⓐ boy

   Ⓑ girl

   Ⓒ mutt

   Ⓓ stray

3 Will you give me a <u>beverage</u>?

   Ⓐ boost up

   Ⓑ lemonade

   Ⓒ lift

   Ⓓ drink

4 That dress is an <u>unusual</u> color.

   Ⓐ odd

   Ⓑ peculiar

   Ⓒ pretty

   Ⓓ unattractive

5 The fly was <u>annoying</u> the teacher.

   Ⓐ tickling

   Ⓑ irritating

   Ⓒ infuriating

   Ⓓ buzzing

Directions: Choose the word that means the <u>opposite</u> of the word that is underlined.

6 the snow was <u>freezing</u>

   Ⓐ icy

   Ⓑ steep

   Ⓒ scalding

   Ⓓ fluffy

7 <u>investigate</u> a mystery

   Ⓐ ignore

   Ⓑ curious

   Ⓒ check into

   Ⓓ sneak

8 <u>cunning</u> as a fox

   Ⓐ sly

   Ⓑ stupid

   Ⓒ careful

   Ⓓ sleepy

(See page 97 for answer key.)

Multi-Meaning Words

Fourth graders often have fun learning about homonyms (also called multi-meaning words)—words that have the same spelling and pronunciation, but that are different in meaning:

The young woman began to file her nails.

The secretary put the letters in the file.

Younger children can be quite inflexible with such words, but by fourth grade they can easily handle the complexity of multiple meanings in one word.

Keep in Mind. Be sure your child reads the directions carefully when completing sections assessing multi-meaning words in standardized tests. It's easy to get confused about what the directions are asking for.

Practice Skill: Multi-Meaning Words

Directions: In which sentence does the underlined word mean the same as in the sentence above it?

9 Sue held a marshmallow over the <u>fire</u>.

   (A) The boss will <u>fire</u> the worker for coming in late.

   (B) Tim and his friends built a huge <u>fire</u> at their campsite.

   (C) The wild stallion had <u>fire</u> in his eyes.

   (D) The teacher will <u>fire</u> you with excitement.

10 The little boy climbed into his grandmother's <u>lap</u>.

   (A) The kitten liked to <u>lap</u> his milk.

   (B) Gerry ran another <u>lap</u> around the gym.

   (C) Larry heard the stream <u>lap</u> the banks.

   (D) I love to hold the puppy on my <u>lap</u>.

Directions: Read the two sentences with the blanks. Choose the word that fits into both sentences.

11 Sam didn't know he had a hole in his _____.
The young girl would never _____ of riding her pony.

   (A) time

   (B) tire

   (C) lot

   (D) sleep

12 There is no _____ on the moon. Be quiet! The program is about to _____.

   (A) mud

   (B) close

   (C) water

   (D) air

(See page 97 for answer key.)

Words in Context

As your child gets older, you are probably noticing that she is becoming a far more fluent reader who no longer has to struggle with every word. By fourth grade, most children have developed a keen sense of the whole meaning of the combined elements of sentences, and are able to fill in missing elements and detect things that don't belong in the sentence.

What Tests May Ask

Standardized tests will include questions that assess whether your child can understand words in context. Remember to stress to your child that words in context must be carefully read if the true meaning is to be picked up. Make sure your child skims the passage first, reading each sentence carefully and relying on the meaning of the whole sentence to help find the answer.

Practice Skill: Words in Context

Directions: Read the following paragraph and choose the correct word for each numbered blank.

Owning your own horse can be lots of fun, but they are lots of ____(13), too. You must give a horse ___(14)__ and water every day. His mane and ___(15)__ must be brushed, and the ___(16)___ must be cleaned so it stays soft and comfortable to sit on. Owning a horse is a lot of ___(17)__.

13 Ⓐ dirt

    Ⓑ yellow

    Ⓒ work

    Ⓓ anger

14 Ⓐ hay

    Ⓑ vehicles

    Ⓒ expressions

    Ⓓ pie

15 Ⓐ nostrils

    Ⓑ stall

    Ⓒ tail

    Ⓓ pitchfork

16 Ⓐ bunkbed

    Ⓑ saddle

    Ⓒ bridle

    Ⓓ hammock

17 Ⓐ motivation

    Ⓑ versatility

    Ⓒ responsibility

    Ⓓ support

(See page 97 for answer key.)

Word Study

By the time your child gets to fourth grade, she will have learned that English is really a blend of words from many languages from around the world, but based especially on Latin. Under-standing some of the history of words she uses every day can help her understand the word itself.

What Tests May Ask

Most standardized tests will include some multiple-choice questions asking about word origins. In most cases, your child will be asked to choose the correct meaning of a word given its original form. Explain to your child that figuring out the origins of some words can get confusing if she's in a hurry. Many of the words given on a standardized test will sound very similar. Have her slow down, sound out the word to herself, and try rephrasing the example.

Practice Skill: Word Study

Directions: Choose the correct derived meaning for the following foreign words.

18 Which of these words probably comes from the Middle English <u>tollen</u> meaning "to entice"?

    Ⓐ told

    Ⓑ toll

    Ⓒ tale

    Ⓓ till

19 Which of these words comes from the Old English <u>scimerian</u> meaning "to shine"?

    Ⓐ salad

    Ⓑ sin

    Ⓒ shimmer

    Ⓓ sack

20 Which of these words comes from the Latin <u>dentalis</u> meaning "tooth"?

Ⓐ dental

Ⓑ dangle

Ⓒ derange

Ⓓ dawn

(See page 97 for answer key.)

CHAPTER 3

Reading Comprehension

Reading comprehension tests a child's general ability to understand what a story or article is about and what the author is trying to say. Reading comprehension involves more than just understanding the facts of the piece; it also means your child must be able to "read between the lines" and infer meaning from the information presented, a far more sophisticated type of reading skill than was required in the early elementary grades.

In the fourth grade, your child's job is to deepen his comprehension skills and fluency so that he will be able to move on to even more challenging books in the future.

What Your Fourth Grader Should Be Learning

By now, you're probably amazed at what a fluent reader the typical fourth grader can be. This is the year when your child starts reading to learn, not learning to read. If your fourth grader loves to read, you may be amazed at the number of books he's devouring; "series books" are often high on the list.

Most fourth graders can now read confidently and fluently without stumbling, and should be able to answer straightforward questions about what they've read. But by fourth grade, children are able to do much more. Don't be surprised if your child can now begin to think about what he's reading and predict what may happen next in the story. He should be able to discuss and summarize the main points of the plot, the main characters and what they did, and how the setting may influence the story.

Even more important, your child is now beginning to flex his inferential muscles—that is, to be able to predict and draw conclusions about the author's writing using only veiled hints the author has supplied. He's learning how to tell the difference between fact and opinion and to make observations about the author's intent and motivation as he goes on to be a more critical reader.

In many school districts, fourth graders begin to discuss different writing genres, including mystery, nonfiction, fantasy, myths and legends, autobiography, historical fiction, and poetry.

What Tests May Ask

Standardized tests of reading comprehension for fourth graders include questions on critical reading, inferential comprehension (making educated guesses about what the author meant by reading between the lines), and literal comprehension (basic understanding of a story).

It's not enough to be able to simply understand the vocabulary of a piece of writing; the fourth-grade student is expected to go beyond and dig out the meat of the story. Tests assess the ability to do this through multiple-choice questions by asking students what details are included in the story and what is not included. Students may be asked to select topic sentences and possible story titles, and to differentiate between plot, character, mood, and setting.

What You and Your Child Can Do

Even as your child becomes a confident reader himself, this is not the time to drop the reading ball at your house. In fact, studies suggest that fourth grade is the critical time for developing *permanent* good readers, because up to a third of all children who had been interested in reading up to this point suddenly stall out and stop progressing in this area. The more you can be a good reading model for your child, and encourage daily reading practice at home, the better.

Magazines. Subscribe to age-appropriate magazines such as *Junior Scholastic, Highlights for Children, Stone Soup,* or *American Girl.* Your child may become fascinated with things he never suspected would interest him.

Newspapers. If you let your child see you reading newspapers for pleasure, he'll want to begin to do the same. Point out short articles in the newspaper that you think would interest him; don't just stop on the comics page. With your encouragement, he may feel grown-up enough to bypass the children's page and delve into a science or natural history article that interests him. If he has trouble reading the articles, help him. Enjoy reading together.

Books to Go. We all seem to spend a lot of time in the car running children on errands and trips. Keep a book in the backseat for these times, and have your child read to you as you drive.

Library Visits. As your child gets older, schedule regular trips to the library. Give your child privacy once you get there. By this age your child should have his own library card, which can be a first important step in learning responsibility.

As you wait to check out your books, ask your child to make some predictions. What does he think the book is about? What does he think will happen?

Get Advice. Encourage your child to read books that require him to understand characters, appreciate suspense, and anticipate action. Ask your child's teacher, school librarian, and the children's librarian at your local library for recommendations for series that children this age seem to enjoy. The *Harry Potter* books have an enormous following, as do some of the books on *Star Wars* characters. These and similar books emphasize character and plot development and, although they are at an easy enough level for children to understand them, allow children to anticipate plot and understand the main ideas.

Don't Jump In. At this age, if your child is reading out loud and stumbles on a word, don't step in and correct him. If he doesn't know a word, have him skip the word and read on, and then come back to it. See if he can puzzle out its meaning that way.

Try Picture Books. Don't assume picture books are only for young readers. More and more authors are creating more complex picture books for older readers, such as *Jumanji* by Chris Van Allsburg or Allen Say's *Grandfather's Journey.*

Share. Talk about the books you're reading with your child; ideally, you should chat with each other about your books. Point out to him what you like about your selection, what you think the author might be trying to get across, or what you guess might happen next.

Reading Level. At this age, your child may occasionally choose a book that you know is several grades lower than his current reading level. Don't worry; it's natural. What's most important is that your child enjoys reading. Sometimes easier books simply tell a good story that intrigues your child. As long as your child chooses some books appropriate to his age level, try not to worry about occasional easy readers that show up in his stack of for-fun reading.

Critical Reading

You may not realize it, but every time you pick up a book and read, you're silently asking yourself questions about it as you go along. However, some people ask better questions than others. In fourth grade, children are usually taught a variety of questions to ask themselves to boost comprehension, including:

- What's the author's point?
- What is this story about?
- What's going to happen next?
- What connections can I find?
- What conclusions can I draw?

These are also the questions that most standardized tests focus on in assessing how well your child can read and understand what he reads.

What's the Author's Point?

Most standardized tests are designed to assess whether your child has gotten the author's point. Why did Laura Ingalls Wilder write about her childhood on the prairie? Because she knew that her experiences as a settler in the early American West would otherwise be forgotten. Why do authors write stories? To tug at our heartstrings, or make us laugh? Reveal injustice or praise a hero? Knowing the kind of book the author intends to write also affects how we read it—slow or fast, for fun or to learn something.

What Tests May Ask

Standardized tests may include questions on finding the author's purpose by asking students to define genre, or by presenting a list of possible ideas and having children choose which seems closest to the author's point.

What You and Your Child Can Do

Pick one of your child's favorite (but brief!) stories—a short legend or fable, such as the *Three Billy Goats Gruff*—and ask him to tell the story from a different point of view, perhaps from the troll's perspective, not the goat's. Or ask him to tell the *Cinderella* story from the point of view of one of the ugly stepsisters, or *Robin Hood* from the sheriff's perspective.

To boost critical thinking skills, you can work on this area during your nightly reading. Ask questions like:

What do you think will happen next?

Why do you think this character took this action rather than doing something else?

What do you think the main character would think about your world? How do you know that?

It's also important to share your own critical thinking with your child, so he can understand that one of the reasons we read other author's writing is to get their opinions. Many children never have the chance to hear adults discuss information they read about.

Compare and Contrast

It's important that your child be able to compare and contrast things he finds in stories. In *The Dark Is Rising* by Susan Cooper, how is the main character, Will Stanton, different from the others? How is he the same? Would you say that Will was a friend or an enemy of The Dark?

Standardized tests can't ask open-ended questions about comparisons and contrasting story elements, but they may ask your child direct questions requiring him to classify a character or choose how two characters or settings are alike or different.

Helping your child make connections and contrast story elements as he goes along will make him a better, more critical reader. Ask him "what would happen" questions about every day life; What would happen if you went to school and your teacher didn't appear in class? What would happen if you came home early from school and no one was home? What would happen if everybody suddenly stopped obeying traffic laws?

Sum Up or Sequence

It may seem simple to you, but the ability to read a passage and then summarize it is not an inborn skill. It takes practice and involves an understanding of the main points and an ability to put those main points in sequence. In earlier grades, when asked to summarize, most children will give you an almost complete retelling of the reading sample. By fourth grade, your child should be able to pick out key elements and put them together in a logical sequence.

Standardized tests assess this skill by asking your child to read a selection and then pick out which comes first, or by asking your child to sequence a series of statements.

Summing up takes practice. Try to make it fun: Get one of your child's favorite books and ask him to make up a newspaper headline from it:

- Boy Wizard Triumphs Over Evil! (J. K. Rowling's *Harry Potter and the Sorcerer's Stone*)

- Girl Stranded on Alien Planet! (Madeleine L'Engle's *A Wrinkle in Time*)

Practice Skill: Critical Reading

Directions: Read the following questions and choose the answer you think is correct.

1 Which of these sentences states a fact?

   Ⓐ It makes more sense to build housing developments on farmland.

   Ⓑ Farms provide vegetables, fruits, and meat for people to consume.

   Ⓒ Farms pollute the environment because they use too much pesticide.

   Ⓓ Big cities with sparkling lights are prettier than empty farmland.

2 Which of these statements could have appeared in a magazine ad?

   Ⓐ Wolves are an endangered species.

   Ⓑ Smarties are the best candy in town!

   Ⓒ Sharon was the best speller in the class.

   Ⓓ It's going to be a long, hot summer.

Directions: Read the following story, and then answer the questions that follow.

The wind moaned as the wind tossed the trees wildly in the black night sky. The hair on the back of Sharon's neck prickled as a loose shutter banged against the old house. Suddenly, the lights flickered and went out!

3 What part of the story does this passage tell about?

   Ⓐ the characters

   Ⓑ the plot

   Ⓒ the mood

   Ⓓ the setting

4 Sam is reading a book called <u>New Kid at School</u>. Which of these sentences is the first one of the story?

(A) The tall, thin boy in the mis-matched socks stood uncertainly in the doorway of the classroom, alone amidst a sea of returning fifth graders.

(B) The bell rang for recess and we all flew out the door.

(C) Miss Jones read us our assignment and we closed our books.

(D) It was too hot in the classroom to read, so we all filed outside to study under the tree.

(See page 97 for answer key.)

Literal Comprehension

Literal comprehension refers to how well your child understands straightforward questions about information contained in a piece of writing. Good readers constantly draw conclusions about what they read as they go along.

Fourth graders are now quite fluent readers, capable of devouring a wide variety of genres: nonfiction, mystery, fantasy, poetry, plays, auto-biography, historical fiction, and folktales or legends. Your child should be able to read well with expression and without stumbling over many words.

What Tests May Ask

In standardized tests of literal comprehension, your child will probably be given a brief passage to read followed by a series of questions he must answer about the passage. The questions are usually simple, straightforward ones about the story setting, tone, and chain of events. These tests may also ask your child what *wasn't* in the story. Standardized tests also assess your child's ability to reach conclusions about a passage of writing by asking him to tell the difference between fact and opinion, or by asking questions about why a character did what he did.

Learning how to summarize and make conclusions, how to distinguish between the main points of a piece and the details, how to tell fact from opinion, and how to sequence, will make your child a better reader and writer. If you want your child to understand why characters do what they do, he must be able to draw conclusions.

What You and Your Child Can Do

Play the game of conclusions: "We're not having pancakes today because...." or "We're going to get a new car because...." Make it into a game and encourage funny answers. Children often make conclusions but don't recognize that this is what they're doing. Ask them to make a list of conclusions they came up with each day. Help them with the first two or three, and then they should get the idea. (You listened to the weather report and then chose to carry an umbrella. What did you conclude after listening to the weather?) Ask them to come up with a list of careers that require the person to make conclusions, such as lawyers or judges (when they hear a case) or a veterinarian (making a diagnosis of a sick pet).

Practice Skill: Literal Comprehension

Directions: Read the passage below. Find the best answer to the questions that follow.

<u>The Mystery of the Ivory Charm</u> (by Carolyn Keene)

Nancy sat in her father's law office, waiting for him to finish a long-distance call. As he cradled the telephone, she said, "What's up, Dad? Another mystery?"

Mr. Drew nodded and smiled. "It concerns a member of a wild animal show."

"Man or beast?" his eighteen-year-old

daughter teased, her blue eyes twinkling.

"Maybe both," the tall, handsome lawyer replied. "That's for you to find out."....

As soon as she reached home, Nancy phoned her friends Bess and George, who were eager to attend the wild animal show. Little Tommy from down the street was also ecstatic over the idea. He came up to the Drew house at once to show his delight by doing a series of somersaults.

5 The setting at the outset of this story is:

Ⓐ school

Ⓑ diner

Ⓒ law office

Ⓓ bedroom

6 What was the first action Nancy took when she got home?

Ⓐ She went to play with Tommy.

Ⓑ She called her father.

Ⓒ She called Bess and George.

Ⓓ She ate a snack.

7 Which of these is NOT explained in the story?

Ⓐ who Bess and George are

Ⓑ how Nancy got home

Ⓒ how old Nancy is

Ⓓ what Nancy's father does for a living

(See page 97 for answer key.)

Inferential Comprehension

Your fourth grader should be comfortable not just in recognizing words, but in understanding the stories he reads both from what an author says and from the hints embedded in a story that your child now has the sophistication to pick up.

As soon as your child reaches for a book, he's making a prediction about it. Will it be happy or sad, full of facts or full of fantasy? As he learns to predict what is going to happen once he starts reading, he is also developing the ability to make inferences as a way to go beyond "just the facts."

When you go to the library with your child, don't just grab the latest *Goosebumps* and head home. Walk up and down the shelves with your child and look at the different genres. Talk about why an author might have written in a particular style.

What Tests May Ask

Standardized tests of inferential comprehension present a sample bit of text followed by a series of questions that require a more thoughtful evaluation of the passage. Students may be asked to predict what would happen next, or to manipulate the information to come up with answers to novel questions.

What You and Your Child Can Do

When listening to the weather or the evening news or reading the newspaper, ask your child to predict what the next day's story will be on the same subject. Then check the next day to see how close he came. Tear out a page from one of your child's old magazines and ask your child to come up with text that fills in the missing parts.

Practice Skill: Inferential Comprehension

Directions: Read the passage and answer the questions that follow.

The last of the giant dinosaurs disappeared from the earth more than 65 million years ago, but we are still learning more about them every day from the dusty bones they left behind. The word <u>dinosaur</u> comes from two Greek words that mean "terrible lizard," and the name fits! For example, the triceratops was massive—up to 25 feet long with a large, bony frill around his neck and three long, pointed horns on his face, some almost three feet long. The baryonyx had strange crocodile-like teeth and enormous claws, a foot long, that it used to snare fish. While no one knows for sure what caused the dinosaurs to die out, many people think that, for whatever reason, their environment changed too radically for the dinosaurs to survive. As the climate changed and food died out, the dinosaurs died off, leaving the world to the mammals who were much better adapted to survive.

8 Which of the following would be the best title for this story?

Ⓐ The Life of the Baryonyx

Ⓑ The History of Dinosaurs

Ⓒ Life in Times Past

Ⓓ Giant Monsters of the Earth

9 Which of the following is NOT a fact from the story?

Ⓐ Dinosaurs probably looked terrible.

Ⓑ Dinosaurs lived in Egypt.

Ⓒ Baryonyx ate fish.

Ⓓ We learn about dinosaurs from their bones.

10 You would probably understand the word "dinosaur" if you could speak

Ⓐ Greek

Ⓑ French

Ⓒ Swahili

Ⓓ Latin

11 If the demise of the dinosaur happened as scientists think it did, what do you think might happen on earth if there was a sudden massive environmental change?

Ⓐ The polar ice caps might melt.

Ⓑ Many plants and animals would die.

Ⓒ It would rain for months on end.

Ⓓ The earth would tilt on its axis.

Directions: Read the following letter to the editor. Choose the best answers to the questions that follow.

To the Editor:

I read with great dismay the plans that the county has developed to bring Rt. 325 through Smithtown's outlying farms. At the rate we're going, there isn't going to be any farmland left! If the county thinks that we need more roads, why don't they just widen the main road through town?

Some of our farmers have been living on their land for the past 150 years. There is nowhere for them to go and no land they can afford to buy if you continue with your plans to bring this road through. Of course, farmers don't have the sort of big money they can contribute to election campaigns. I know that these farms will bring lots more money as developed land and businesses than they do as farms, which means more money for the county and for the developers' pockets. But there are some things that are worth more than lining the pockets of politicians!

It's time we farmers all got together and made our voices heard—in the voting booth!

12 The writer of the letter is probably:

Ⓐ a developer

Ⓑ a county official

Ⓒ a farmer

Ⓓ a builder

13 What do you think the letter writer will do in November?

     (A) He will ignore election day.

     (B) He will vote for the current county officials.

     (C) He will run for election.

     (D) He will vote against county officials.

14 What is the tone of this letter?

     (A) bitter

     (B) happy

     (C) pleased

     (D) funny

(See page 97 for answer key.)

CHAPTER 4

Language Mechanics

When we think of language mechanics, we're really talking about old-fashioned grammar and punctuation. Fourth grade is the time for putting the final touches to your child's understanding of the correct way to use words and how they fit together in sentences. At this age, your child's teacher will expect her to prepare assignments that demonstrate a solid grasp of grammar, punctuation, and capitalization.

While in some districts the teaching of traditional grammar is still controversial, many educators believe in—and standardized tests still cover—the basics of grammar and language mechanics. Indeed, a child who is to read and write effectively in English must understand the underlying concepts.

Language mechanics also includes punctuation and capitalization, as fourth graders further hone their reading and writing skills. Your child will probably be working on punctuation and capitalization on a daily basis in her classroom. Check with your child's teacher to be sure that punctuation and capitalization are being taught. If your district doesn't emphasize this area, you need to step in and help your child.

What Your Fourth Grader Should Be Learning

In the fourth grade, your child will continue her study of English grammar; she should be able to correctly identify and use the parts of speech such as nouns, verbs, adjectives, adverbs, and prepositions. Punctuation continues to be important; she should be able to correctly use the comma, dash, apostrophe, quotation marks, and italics, and should be able to capitalize correctly both the beginnings of sentences and proper nouns.

Some fourth-grade teachers cover these topics the old-fashioned way, with grammar books and worksheets, while others include it as part of the writing process. This is often fairly easy, because fourth graders typically enjoy writing letters to pen pals or friends, and enjoy writing away for free items.

What Tests May Ask

Expect to find a wide range of questions focusing on punctuation, capitalization, and grammar on standardized tests in the fourth grade. Punctuation questions will include knowing when to use periods, commas, quotation marks, and exclamation marks and identifying incorrectly placed marks. Students will also be expected to know how to capitalize proper nouns, the first words of sentences, and titles of books and movies, and to recognize all the major parts of speech.

What You and Your Child Can Do

If your district is teaching the mechanics of English, you can simply go over your child's homework and classwork sent home daily or weekly. Look for your child's mistakes and analyze them.

The goal is for your child to apply capitals and punctuation and use correct grammar so automatically that she'll never have to give it a moment's thought as she writes, freeing her to be truly creative.

If your school district doesn't emphasize capitalization, punctuation, and grammar in fourth grade, you'll need to work on these areas at home. Your child will be expected to know these skills on standardized tests and in college or a career, so you'll need to teach her yourself if she can't learn it any other way.

You may blanch at the idea of teaching grammar at the dinner table, but the concepts aren't complex—capitals, periods, commas, and quotation marks. Your goal is to make sure your child is capable of writing a correct, coherent sentence.

Write! Encourage your child to write. This is good practice, but it's also a good way to brush up on grammar, punctuation, and capitalization. Suggest she write a play (fourth graders tend to love to perform) for her class, and get everyone to take part.

Be Supportive. When your child asks you to look at her work, praise the ideas—the content of what she has written—before you step in and start editing the grammar or punctuation.

Keep a Diary. Encourage your child to keep a diary (but don't look at it unless she invites you to do so). There are attractive journals and diaries at stationery stores and bookstores, and they make nice gifts for children.

Capitalization

By fourth grade, capitalization should be almost automatic, including capitalizing names, titles, programs, proper nouns, and so on. Capitaliza-

tion and punctuation are becoming important parts of the curriculum in many fourth-grade classrooms, now that many schools are experiencing a swing away from a pure whole language approach to the language arts.

What Tests May Ask

Standardized tests assess capitalization by asking fourth graders to choose the correct capitalized word from a variety of choices. Because standardized tests must currently assess capitalization skills in a way that can be scored by computer, they must rely on children's ability to recognize correct capitalization rather than produce it. While some researchers are developing computer-assisted testing procedures that would require children to enter their own capitalizations, these aren't widely available yet.

What You and Your Child Can Do

Does your child remember to capitalize the start of each sentence? The personal pronoun *I*? The names of proper nouns, such as states, months, and people's names? Titles of people as well as titles of books and movies?

If your child tends to forget what to capitalize, she may simply need a little more practice. The best way to improve is to write—anything! Encourage her to write letters to friends, pen pals, or family members. Have her write a business letter to send away for a toy or some clothes. Ask if she'd like to send a fan letter. Just anything to get her writing. Make sure she writes the envelopes, because a lot of capitalization rules apply.

Practice Skill: Capitalization

Directions: Choose the sentence that shows correct capitalization.

1 Ⓐ I want to go Ice skating in January.

　　Ⓑ Are you going to make Boeuf bordelaise?

　　Ⓒ Jim and Suzy are staying in New York City this year.

　　Ⓓ I think the Sun is shining outside.

2 Ⓐ In the Summer, Sharon will go to Disney World.

　　Ⓑ In the nineteenth century, president Abraham Lincoln gave a famous speech in gettysburg.

　　Ⓒ In January we are going to Windsor Castle to pay a visit to Queen Elizabeth II.

　　Ⓓ come here, Rover!

Punctuation

Just as with capitalization, by fourth grade most children should be fairly comfortable using the punctuation marks, including comma, period, exclamation mark, and quotation mark; many are also using colons and semicolons with aplomb. They should be able to punctuate even complicated compound sentences with ease.

In the early grades, children simply write in one long sentence, never able to distinguish where one idea stops and another begins; they also read passages as one run-on sentence, with no pauses for breath or dramatic effect. By fourth grade, your child should be far more fluent and comfortable with all types of language mechanics.

What Tests May Ask

As with capitalization, the challenge in assessing punctuation skills on standardized tests is in presenting test items in a format that will allow children to answer them on scan sheets used to score them by computer.

At present, we must rely on assessments that test a child's ability to recognize correct and incorrect punctuation when she sees it. Standardized tests frequently present sentences and ask which one of the three or four is punctuated correctly.

Be sure your child notices whether she is to find the **correct** or **incorrect** example in a test question.

What You and Your Child Can Do

Most kids love the computer, so if you can, use it to try to teach punctuation and editing skills. Type a paragraph or more (make it as funny as you can) on the computer, and include lots of punctuation and capitalization errors. Now invite your child to "fix" the paragraph. If you have a grammar or spell checker, let her run that to check her work when she's finished. Youngsters this age often find that working with the computer seems more like fun than like work.

Practice Skill: Punctuation

Directions: Which of these sentences is punctuated correctly?

3 Ⓐ Sally likes ice cream, but, does not like cake.

　　Ⓑ Donald can ride a bicycle but he needs training wheels.

　　Ⓒ Jean washed, and waxed her mother's car.

　　Ⓓ Jennifer washed her hands and dried them on the towel.

4 Ⓐ "I don't care what you're doing, I want you to stop! said father.

Ⓑ Susan added up the cost of the twine, the scissors, and the packet of needles.

Ⓒ Jared ran to get his ball bat and glove.

Ⓓ Are you going to the store!

Directions: Choose where punctuation needs to be added in this sentence.

5 Jim_ran down the_hill carrying his pail,
     A   **B**

shovel_and broom.
   C   **D**

Ⓐ A

Ⓑ B

Ⓒ C

Ⓓ D

6 Susan_was born_on July 3_1976.
     A   **B**   **C** **D**

Ⓐ A

Ⓑ B

Ⓒ C

Ⓓ D

(See page 97 for answer key.)

Parts of Speech

Learning the parts of speech has never been a favorite activity for most children, but it's still important for good writing. Names like "noun" and "predicate" just don't mean anything to a child, and that makes it hard to learn. Moreover, the idea that words can be sorted into categories and can change categories depending on the sentence isn't a simple concept to teach.

For example, the word "tease" has two different functions in the following sentences:

Sam's little brother is a terrible <u>tease</u>.

Mother asked her three children not to <u>tease</u> their sister.

In the first sentence, "tease" is a noun; in the second sentence, it's a verb. It's not always easy for fourth graders to understand how the same word can function as a different part of speech.

What Your Fourth Grader Should Be Learning

Your child should be able to identify nouns, verbs, adjectives, and adverbs, and be able to write using correct agreement between nouns and verbs.

What Tests May Ask

Standardized tests ask the fourth grader to edit sentences for grammatical errors; make sure subject and verb tenses agree; identify different parts of speech in examples; and correctly use past, present, and future verb tenses. Your child will definitely have to identify the simple subjects and simple predicates of sentences, and understand proper noun–verb agreement. Through the correct choice of multiple-choice answers, the tests can assess how well your child understands the basics of good grammar. Understanding and choosing the correct tense and picking out the incorrect tense is also an important part of most tests.

What You and Your Child Can Do

Your fourth grader can learn the parts of speech and that words can change category, provided the teaching is on his level. The more concrete the approach, the better. It's a good idea to be sure the child can identify one part of speech well before you begin introducing others.

Mad Libs. Fourth graders love this game, in which they fill in blanks in a story calling for "noun" or "verb," and then read back the completed story, often with hilarious results. Your child can get quite a lot of practice in coming up with her own parts of speech while having a good time. This is a good game to play in the car.

Word Games. To work on boosting your child's ability to come up with various parts of speech, play this game: Start off with a very brief sentence: "The puppy cried...." Then take turns enlarging the phrase, one word at a time.

YOU: The puppy cried.

CHILD: The *spotted* puppy cried—adjective!

YOU: The spotted puppy cried *sadly*—adverb!

CHILD: The *sleepy* spotted puppy cried sadly—adjective!

The sillier the better, but remember to say which part of speech you've added.

Be a Good Model. If you hear your child making a grammatical mistake, gently correct him and substitute the proper form. Don't expect results overnight; if your child has learned sloppy grammar habits over several years' time, you're not going to be able to break him of the habit in a few days. Modeling consistent good examples of correct spoken and written English will eventually do the trick, however.

Practice Skill: Parts of Speech

Directions: For each sentence, find the underlined part that is the simple subject of the sentence.

7   The <u>dolphins</u> <u>followed</u> our small <u>boat</u>
          A   **B**   **C**
    out to <u>sea</u>.
           D

Ⓐ A

Ⓑ B

Ⓒ C

Ⓓ D

8   <u>Kara</u> <u>skipped</u> down the <u>darkened</u> <u>street</u>.
    A   **B**   **C**   **D**

Ⓐ A

Ⓑ B

Ⓒ C

Ⓓ D

9   <u>Fearing</u> the <u>worst</u>, the <u>pilot</u> came in for
    A   **B**   **C**
    a <u>landing</u>.
      D

Ⓐ A

Ⓑ B

Ⓒ C

Ⓓ D

Directions: For each sentence, find the simple predicate of the sentence.

10   Biscuits, the tiny poodle, jumped into
     A   B   C

   the lake.
        D

   Ⓐ   A

   Ⓑ   B

   Ⓒ   C

   Ⓓ   D

11   Silently, the boat slipped into the
     A   B   C

   winding river.
           D

   Ⓐ   A

   Ⓑ   B

   Ⓒ   C

   Ⓓ   D

(See page 97 for answer key.)

CHAPTER 5

Language Expression

The study of language expression in the fourth grade includes several aspects of English and writing, such as proper usage, writing a good sentence, and the best way of expressing ideas. Language expression also includes knowing how to write a topic sentence, and knowing what to include (and what not to include) in paragraphs.

That may sound fairly easy and basic, but fourth graders still struggle over summarizing (which is needed in order to find a topic sentence), understanding topic sentences, and knowing what makes a paragraph and what doesn't. These skills are all essential for good writing, so it pays to spend some time working with your child.

What Your Fourth Grader Should Be Learning

By the fourth grade, your child should understand how to write a cogent sentence and be able to write good paragraphs with logical sentence construction. Fourth graders are expected to be able to identify topic sentences and to understand that the topic sentence expresses the main point of the paragraph.

This doesn't mean that forming good paragraphs and understanding topic sentences are easy for your child. In many ways, he's still just beginning to put complex thoughts on paper.

But establishing a solid base of language expression now will ensure that his writing skills will improve with each successive grade.

What Tests May Ask

Standardized tests today are designed to measure a student's skills at using words to express ideas, combine simple sentences into complex ones, and identify topic sentences. Although the format of many items in the past has been largely multiple-choice, more and more tests are using items that require students to write a sentence or paragraph, so your child should be prepared to do both.

After your child completes each group of the practice questions here, go over the answers and review all mistakes. Give your child a red pencil and have him correct the mistake on the test. Children find it's helpful to *see* the correction within the actual sentence, and using a different color highlights the correction.

What You and Your Child Can Do

If your child is to use good language expression, the best thing you can do for him is to speak in clear sentences yourself. Children who grow up in a home in which proper English is spoken have far fewer problems in understanding what makes a good sentence, simply because they understand the basics intuitively.

The more your child hears good examples of clear expression, the better. Fourth graders are often quite interested in your own stories. Talk with your children, and expose them to others who talk with them. Explain things to them, talk about your childhood memories of your summers on the lake, tell them about your job or how you care for the family and the home.

Conversation isn't a one-way street—you must also listen to your child. Even in fourth grade, most children are still happy to tell you about their day, how they feel, and especially their opinions. Odds are, they have plenty! Teach them that you value what they have to say.

Practice Skill: Usage

Directions: Choose the word or phrase that best completes the sentence.

1 It is _____ than it was yesterday.

   Ⓐ warmest

   Ⓑ more warmer

   Ⓒ warm

   Ⓓ warmer

2 John _____ to the store tomorrow.

   Ⓐ went

   Ⓑ go

   Ⓒ will go

   Ⓓ going

3 Sarah and _____ went to the party.

   Ⓐ I

   Ⓑ us

   Ⓒ we

   Ⓓ me

Directions: Read the following brief report and use it to answer questions 4–7.

1. Sarah and Jim were both <u>study</u> for a history test. **2.** After Sarah closed her textbook, she read the evening paper, flipped through a magazine, and then <u>watching</u> a TV show before picking up her book to study again. Jim simply studied for his test and then went to bed. **3.** When the two <u>reviews</u> history facts together just before the test, Jim had remembered much more of it. **4.** That's because people who go to sleep right after studying will <u>done</u> better on a test.

4 In sentence 1, <u>study</u> is best written as:

   Ⓐ studying

   Ⓑ studied

   Ⓒ studies

   Ⓓ as it is

5 In sentence 2, <u>watching</u> is best written as:

   Ⓐ watch

   Ⓑ watches

   Ⓒ watched

   Ⓓ as it is

6 In sentence 3, <u>reviews</u> is best written as:

   Ⓐ review

   Ⓑ reviewing

   Ⓒ reviewed

   Ⓓ as it is

7 In sentence 4, <u>done</u> is best written as:

Ⓐ doing

Ⓑ do

Ⓒ does

Ⓓ as it is

(See page 97 for answer key.)

Sentences

By fourth grade, children are expected to write in complete sentences to express a meaningful idea or a complete thought. By this age, your child should understand that sentences have a subject (the *who* or *what* of the sentence) and a predicate or verb (the *action* words that tell what the subject does or is).

To write a good sentence, your child must understand the grammatical structure of the sentence as well. Not only must there be a subject and a predicate, but there must be agreement between the different parts of the sentence: The subject must agree with the verb form, and the verb tense must agree with the sentence's time frame.

In addition, your child will be expected to be able to combine simple sentences into a correctly punctuated complex sentence. It's important to be able to do this, because good writers know how to use a variety of sentence types. One easy way to help your child combine sentences is to teach him to cross out any words that appear more than once and then combine the remaining words into a reasonable sentence. Using commas will help your child combine the sentence.

What Tests May Ask

Standardized tests in fourth grade will present two sentences and ask your child to choose the best way of combining them. Questions will ask for the correct noun or verb in a sentence, or may present a series of sentences and ask your child to choose the best-written of the group. The test will also present a series of sentence fragments and ask your child to pick the one good sentence from the group.

Practice Skill: Sentences

Directions: Choose the answer that is a correctly written sentence.

8 Ⓐ Walking through the trees.

Ⓑ That's a wonderful box you created.

Ⓒ Horse farms on the road.

Ⓓ Jumping through the hoops at the fair.

9 Ⓐ I don't think that her and me can go to the fair today.

Ⓑ Will you help she and me build a snowman?

Ⓒ I and Sarah can finish the chores by ourselves.

Ⓓ Sandy and I will be taking the Valentines to the dance.

10 Ⓐ We were very happily to find out the dog was not hurt.

Ⓑ The doctor came quick down the hospital corridor.

Ⓒ Diana was thrilled to get a puppy for her birthday.

Ⓓ Dinosaurs is now extinct.

Directions: Mark the answer choice that best combines the two sentences.

11 Jordan plays the piano.
   He plays well.

   Ⓐ   Jordan plays piano and the well.

   Ⓑ   Jordan plays piano well.

   Ⓒ   Jordan plays well piano.

   Ⓓ   Well, Jordan plays the piano.

12 Miranda loves to go swimming.
   She has a red swimsuit.

   Ⓐ   Miranda and her swimsuit love to go swimming.

   Ⓑ   Miranda loves to go swimming in her red swimsuit.

   Ⓒ   Miranda love swimming and her suit.

   Ⓓ   Miranda loves to go swimming: she has a red swimsuit.

(See page 97 for answer key.)

Paragraphs

Although children by the fourth grade are writing fairly complex sentences, they don't always know how to break one long essay into separate paragraphs without practice. One part of the problem is knowing how to write a good topic sentence, a subject often included in standardized tests.

The topic sentence is usually the first sentence in a paragraph. It's a good idea to be sure your child can write a simple topic sentence whenever he has to write an essay or paragraph for school. Children often find topic sentences difficult to formulate; they may not understand that the topic sentence is the sentence that expresses the main point of the paragraph. To find a topic sentence, your child simply has to ask himself: "Does this sentence tell the main point of this paragraph? Is it related to every other sentence in the paragraph?" If the answer to both questions is "yes," he's found the topic sentence.

What Tests May Ask

Most standardized tests give students a series of brief paragraphs and then ask questions about those samples. On most standardized tests, students won't come up with their own topic sentences; they simply have to recognize one from a set of examples. (This is a lot easier than writing your own!)

Often, tests give students a topic sentence and then ask for the best "developing" sentence to follow. Students may be asked to find the sentence that doesn't fit in a sample bit of writing, or to reorder sentences in proper sequence. Some tests give students a series of business letters and ask them to choose which is the best for a particular purpose.

What You and Your Child Can Do

One of the best ways to help your child learn how to write a paragraph is to sit with him when he's doing his homework and help him *before* he starts to write. This is especially true for the development of topic sentences.

Often, fourth graders start to write before they have a good idea what they are going to say. Before letting him write a word of the first paragraph, have your child talk about what ideas he wants to include. Jot them down for him if you want, so you don't impede his thought process. Then let him decide which points or ideas he'll include. Finally, have him state a sentence that tells the point of his paragraph. Ask him to sum up what he wants to say in a few words.

When the sentence is well-formed and to the point, have him write it down and then begin his essay. He will be amazed at how much easier it is to write a good paragraph when he's thought about it first.

Practice Skill: Paragraphs

Directions: Read the paragraph below. Find the best topic sentence for the paragraph.

_____. These Costa Rican settlers came mostly from Spain, but they also came from Germany, Britain, and France. Mestizos, or people of Spanish and Native American blood, have increased in number, but they still represent less than 10 percent of the population. The smallest group is the original Native Americans, who probably number fewer than 10,000.

13　Ⓐ　Lots of Costa Ricans are farmers.

　　Ⓑ　Most Costa Ricans are descended from Europeans who arrived in the nineteenth century.

　　Ⓒ　Some Costa Ricans are Native Americans.

　　Ⓓ　Costa Rican people make their living from fishing, forestry, trade and industry.

Directions: Choose the answer that best *develops* the topic sentence below.

14　My uncle Perry has a very unusual hobby.

　　Ⓐ　He works in a large hospital in the x-ray department. He says he loves his job.

　　Ⓑ　He takes a fancy metal detector and explores old creek beds and ancient sites where settlers used to live. He finds all sorts of unusual coins and metal objects from long ago.

　　Ⓒ　He has three children and they live in San Francisco. I have a great time playing with my cousins.

　　Ⓓ　He's lots of fun when he comes to our house. He enjoys telling lots of jokes and plays tricks on my cousins and me.

Directions: Read the paragraphs below and find the sentence that doesn't belong in the paragraph.

1. Taking care of your own horse can be lots of fun—and plenty of responsibility! **2.** You must be sure to offer plenty of fresh hay and clean water. **3.** Grooming your horse every day is also very important! **4.** Lambs can be fun animals to take care of too. **5.** Picking out your horse's feet with a special hoof pick is another important job you must do every day.

15　Ⓐ　sentence one

　　Ⓑ　sentence two

　　Ⓒ　sentence three

　　Ⓓ　sentence four

1. The highest point on the railroad through the Canadian Rockies is Kicking Horse Pass. **2.** The pass was discovered in 1858 by an explorer named James Hector. **3.** His horse kicked him while they were crossing, and that is how the pass got it's name. **4.** Banff National park is Canada's oldest national park.

16　Ⓐ　sentence one

　　Ⓑ　sentence two

　　Ⓒ　sentence three

　　Ⓓ　sentence four

Directions: Read the paragraph below and then answer questions 17 and 18.

1. Kara loved to go visit her Aunt Barbara at her summer home in Maine. **2.** In Maine, the two of them can go windsurfing on the large lake by her aunt's home. **3.** Windsurfing is a fun sport and easy to learn. **4.** Canoes are safe if you don't stand up in them. **5.** They also like to go canoeing in her aunt's large green canoe. **6.** Moose come to drink at twilight.

17 Where is the best place for sentence 4?

Ⓐ between sentences 1 and 2

Ⓑ between sentences 5 and 6

Ⓒ between sentences 3 and 4

Ⓓ where it is now

18 Which sentence should be left out of this paragraph?

Ⓐ sentence 1

Ⓑ sentence 2

Ⓒ sentence 4

Ⓓ sentence 6

(See page 97 for answer key.)

CHAPTER 6

Spelling and Study Skills

Long gone are the days when you could spell in front of your child and not be understood. By fourth grade, your child should be able to complete a piece of writing and have most of the words spelled correctly.

That doesn't mean you should expect perfect spelling from your fourth grader; after all, that's something many adults still haven't achieved. But most schools continue to believe that teaching spelling is important, and standardized tests still devote time to the assessment of spelling.

Fourth grade seems to be that watershed year when children decide whether they are "just naturally good spellers" or not, and that designation often remains with you for life. In fact, no one knows why some people seem to be "born" good spellers while others are unable to spell well.

Some researchers believe spelling is an inborn skill for some people, requiring almost no effort. After one or two exposures to a word, these people seem to be able to memorize letters in order and retain that memory permanently. Other children seem unable to spell no matter what they do. Even after drilling with the words all week, they may not be able to spell correctly on the test—or if they manage that, they often forget the words soon afterward.

If your child is not one of the born spellers, there are plenty of ways you can work with her to boost her performance. This chapter includes helpful techniques to use with children who need help in spelling.

In the second half of this chapter, we discuss study skills, focusing on the areas that standardized tests frequently include:

- reading maps,
- outlines, and
- dictionary, glossary, index, and table of contents work.

What Your Fourth Grader Should Be Learning

By fourth grade, your child should be able to spell most of the 1,000 most frequently used words in English and begin to edit her own work for misspelled words, either on a computer or by using a dictionary. Fourth graders should know some spelling rules from English: that we double the final consonant before adding "-ing," that "i" comes before "e" except after the letter "c," and that the final consonant is doubled before adding "y," but not before adding "ey." She should also know how to use a dictionary, read maps, and find information using a table of contents, glossary, or index.

What You and Your Child Can Do

By the time their children are in fourth grade, most parents have developed a routine for teaching spelling. Some parents simply call out the words and have the child spell back to them. Others ask their child to write the words as a way of committing them to memory. Some parents use a combination of methods. If these methods work for you and your child has no problems with spelling, skip the next section.

Analyze Errors. If your child doesn't spell easily, you may find that the traditional methods mentioned have never worked. In this case, you should look at your child's spelling tests for the last few weeks. If she can spell the words on the test, but misspells them the week after in her writing, analyze her errors. Is she an inventive speller? This is the child who spells the word exactly as it sounds: *nodee* for the word *naughty*. Or does your child try to spell the word as it looks but make errors of omission ("wistle") or errors of sequence ("whistel")?

Emphasize Spelling Patterns. Children who make these kinds of mistakes need more study of English spelling patterns. While many people stress the irregular spellings of English words (like "through" or "know"), most English words fall into regular patterns. Helping your child to recognize these patterns should improve her spelling.

It's best if your spelling program doesn't consist of words taken from the stories being read in language arts that week. Spelling words should be grouped by spelling patterns, not by meaning. Poor spellers need frequent exposure to spelling patterns and they need to be told explicitly about the patterns they will find in words. Don't expect a poor speller to automatically notice that "fudge," "wedge," and "lodge" all have a "d" that you can hardly hear when the word is spoken. If they noticed these things on their own, they would be good spellers!

Homework Checks. As you go over your child's written homework, point out any misspellings, because the longer you allow your child to practice incorrect spelling, the harder it will be for her to learn correct spelling. As you check your child's homework and school papers,

make a list of words your child routinely misspells. She will probably routinely misspell the same words and make the same errors (usually one or two letters) in each difficult word.

Make note cards with those words, with the routinely misspelled letters capitalized. Go over the "challenging" words from time to time. For example, if your child routinely misspells the word "rhythm" as "*rhthymn*," write it on the note card as rhYTHM.

Word Lists. Most state education departments publish lists of recommended words that children at each grade level should be able to read and spell. These lists can be helpful resources because they're generally designed to match the vocabulary children in each grade encounter in school, and the level of vocabulary tested in the standardized tests each state uses.

Ask your child's teacher for a copy of your state's fourth-grade word list. (If the teacher doesn't know about the list, write to the instructional division of your state department of public instruction and ask whether there is a list and if they will send you a copy.)

Memory Aids. Sometimes poor spellers simply have trouble memorizing. There are all sorts of memory tricks you can teach your child.

Practice! Sometimes, all it takes to help your child is a little more time spent on spelling practice. Instead of waiting to begin studying for Friday's test on Monday, ask the teacher to send the word list home for the weekend; you can start studying on Sunday and have an extra day to practice.

Most children can spell some of the words on their spelling list. Look over the words and check off the ones you think your child knows already. Practice these only a few times, and if you're right, don't keep drilling on those. Instead, concentrate on words that your child doesn't know. It will be much less frustrating to concentrate on five or six tricky words than to continually drill your child on 15 words, most of which he knows.

Sound. Coming up with different pronunciations may help your child spell the word. Most people who misspell "regular" can get the first part right but end the word in "er" instead of "ar." So emphasize the word: "Reg-u-LAR."

Break It Down. If your child spells "buckle" as "bukle," take the word apart and break it down for him. If he can spell "buck," say to your child: "Look, there's a buck in buckle. The cowboy, who rode the bucking horse, wore a buckle." The funnier or sillier you can make the sentence, the more memorable it will be.

Colorize. If you can link a problem spelling word with something visual, your child will be able to remember the word more easily. Tell your child to think of the word in a vivid color; imagine the word "famous" written in a bright orange. Some people can remember words better when they are linked to a color.

Sing. Add music whenever possible. If your child misspells central "centeral," you can have him sing the correct spelling to a common tune, such as *Twinkle, Twinkle*. His old way of spelling won't fit the pattern of the song, and spelling to a song helps embed it in memory.

Review. When the spelling test is over and even if your child has done well, she may not retain the word in memory if you don't occasionally review the word. Keep a list of old troublesome words—the ones most likely to be used again—and go back over them from time to time. Remember, standardized spelling tests will include the words that she once spelled right and may have forgotten. Tricky words like "through" and "rhythm" will be needed again, but words like "rhinoceros" can probably be put aside.

Reward. Don't forget the value of rewards when it comes to learning. Set aside a time to review spelling a few nights a week. When the words are spelled correctly, give a small treat, such as a night off from setting the table. After all, adults don't work without rewards, and a small recognition of a job well done is a fine incentive to keep on working.

Spelling

Whether your child is a born speller or has spelling difficulties, it's a good idea to spend some time with general spelling boosters for all children. Here are some fun, general ways to help your child work on spelling.

Scrabble. Games like Scrabble (or Scrabble Jr. for struggling spellers) provide an excellent way to boost confidence in spelling and vocabulary at the same time.

Hangman. While Scrabble can be lots of fun, it's not always convenient to play it unless you're at home, where the Scrabble board is. Hangman is a wonderful spelling game you can play anywhere, anytime, as long as you have a piece of scratch paper and a pencil. You can play it in the car, in a restaurant while waiting for your meal, or in the doctor's office waiting for an appointment. It's also a good way of teaching language mechanics, because you can discuss vowel rules and strategies that may help enhance spelling skills.

Crossword Puzzles. Completing crossword puzzles aimed at the fourth-grade level can be a fun way of reinforcing spelling skills.

Practice Skill: Spelling

Directions: Read each word and select the word that has a spelling error. If there is no mistake, select the last choice.

1   Ⓐ   pioneer

    Ⓑ   nervus

    Ⓒ   welcome

    Ⓓ   accurate

    Ⓔ   no mistakes

2 Ⓐ simply

   Ⓑ exact

   Ⓒ islend

   Ⓓ location

   Ⓔ no mistakes

3 Ⓐ honored

   Ⓑ unfair

   Ⓒ purchace

   Ⓓ harmless

   Ⓔ no mistakes

4 Ⓐ beyond

   Ⓑ mountain

   Ⓒ oppose

   Ⓓ praise

   Ⓔ no mistakes

Directions: For questions 5–8, read each phrase. One of the underlined words is not spelled correctly for the way it's used in the phrase. Choose the word that is NOT spelled correctly for the way it's used.

5 Ⓐ <u>though</u> the door

   Ⓑ <u>heard</u> a sound

   Ⓒ sun <u>burn</u>

   Ⓓ <u>two</u> eyes

6 Ⓐ <u>herd</u> sheep

   Ⓑ wooden <u>nickel</u>

   Ⓒ <u>there</u> car

   Ⓓ <u>freight</u> train

7 Ⓐ outdoor <u>picnic</u>

   Ⓑ hurt <u>knee</u>

   Ⓒ <u>blue</u> hat

   Ⓓ <u>knew</u> dress

8 Ⓐ bad <u>weather</u>

   Ⓑ elephant's <u>tusk</u>

   Ⓒ heavy <u>lode</u>

   Ⓓ honey <u>bee</u>

Directions: For questions 9–12, find the word that is spelled correctly and best fits in the blank.

9 That flower has a wonderful _____.

   Ⓐ sent

   Ⓑ scente

   Ⓒ scent

   Ⓓ seint

10 Are you _____ that you left your homework at school?

   Ⓐ awair

   Ⓑ awar

   Ⓒ aware

   Ⓓ awear

11 We were both _____ to see you.

   Ⓐ hapy

   Ⓑ happie

   Ⓒ hippy

   Ⓓ happy

12 Can we come _____?

    Ⓐ   to

    Ⓑ   two

    Ⓒ   too

    Ⓓ   toe

(See page 97 for answer key.)

Study Skills

For many children, fourth grade marks the beginning of *serious* school, with much more homework than ever before in more complicated subjects. As your child's school career begins to intensify, she needs to learn how to apply basic reading skills and strategies.

Fourth grade is an important time for facts, and most children this age love to learn them. Your child should be discovering the basics of research, including how to use a dictionary, using guide words at the top of the page to locate entries. She should already know how to alphabetize to the third or fourth letter; now, in fourth grade, she will learn how to use various features of nonfiction books, including:

- table of contents,
- glossary,
- index, and
- appendix.

You will also most likely notice more work in maps and atlases coming home, as your child begins to learn how to decode these specialized reference tools.

What You and Your Child Can Do

Standardized tests don't usually include many items about study skills in fourth grade, but there will be some. Your child may already be using a dictionary and glossary in her homework assignments, but you might want to test her on this at home to make sure. The next time you're looking through her history book, give her a name and see if she looks it up using the index or table of contents. Ask her what the appendix is used for.

Visit your local library, and introduce your child to all the rich resources there. By teaching her how to find what she's looking for, and how to ask for help from the librarians when she can't, you're giving her valuable skills she'll use for the rest of her life.

Practice Skill: Study Skills

dry		duchess

Directions: Look at the picture of the dictionary page. "Dry" and "duchess" are the two guide words at the top of the page. Answer questions 13 and 14 using this dictionary page.

13 Which word would be found on this page?

    Ⓐ   drug

    Ⓑ   drudge

    Ⓒ   ease

    Ⓓ   dual

14 Which word would be found on this page?

    Ⓐ   drove

    Ⓑ   drum

    Ⓒ   ducat

    Ⓓ   determined

Directions: For questions 15–17, choose the word or name that would come first if they were arranged in alphabetical order.

15 Ⓐ patch

    Ⓑ pancake

    Ⓒ pincher

    Ⓓ pins

16 Ⓐ Smith, Fiona

    Ⓑ Taylor, Elise

    Ⓒ Hutchins, Kara

    Ⓓ Abel, Kate

17 Ⓐ Miller, Katie

    Ⓑ Miller, Catherine

    Ⓒ Miller, Wanda

    Ⓓ Miller, Joseph

Directions: Choose the best answer for the following questions.

18 Which of these books would you use to find where Portugal is located?

    Ⓐ telephone book

    Ⓑ calendar

    Ⓒ atlas

    Ⓓ cookbook

19 If you wanted to find all the pages that mention anything about golden retrievers in a book on dogs, where would you look in the book?

    Ⓐ table of contents

    Ⓑ appendix

    Ⓒ index

    Ⓓ glossary

20 Where is the best place to find a brief biography of Abraham Lincoln?

    Ⓐ atlas

    Ⓑ calendar

    Ⓒ encyclopedia

    Ⓓ dictionary

(See page 97 for answer key.)

CHAPTER 7

Math Concepts

"Basic math concepts" refers to the building blocks on which more advanced mathematical procedures are built. For example, in order to add multidigit numbers, you must understand place value. Being comfortable with the building blocks makes learning math less a chore and more fun.

Learning the basic principles behind math concepts will reveal a consistent, predictable order to the world. But no matter how easily your child learns math, there is no way to avoid rote memorization and practice in learning math concepts. We can try to make the process as painless and as child-friendly as possible, but we only learn math concepts when we make a focused effort to learn them and set aside time to practice them.

What Your Fourth Grader Should Be Learning

Fourth graders continue work in addition and subtraction while adding more work on number concepts, place value, fractions, and decimals. Those who remain weak in math facts should spend some time brushing up, including more work on multiplication tables. Fourth graders also spend time learning to estimate; compare and order whole numbers; factor numbers; add, subtract, and reduce fractions; use a number line; and add, subtract, and convert fractions.

What You and Your Child Can Do

If you want to help your child, it's important that you learn the way your child is being taught. Although there are usually many different ways to solve math problems, it's best if you follow the method in your child's math book. Math is hard enough for children without trying to teach them how to solve problems in a different way. When it comes to math concepts, it's not a good idea to invent your own games for the car or at the dinner table. Instead, you'll do best if you stick closely to your child's math book. If you can't figure out the process, call the teacher. Most teachers will be happy to help you in your efforts to work with your child at home.

What Tests May Ask

As a way of testing the extent to which your fourth grader has understood math concepts, standardized tests measure how well your child can estimate; compare and order whole numbers; factor numbers; add, subtract, and reduce fractions; use a number line; and add, subtract, and convert fractions. Questions may ask your child to fill in a missing number in a pattern, to rank numbers according to size, and to write numbers in both standard and expanded form.

Numeration

Numeration refers to the system of numbers that we use, a system that follows a prescribed sequence with certain properties. A number is really a symbol that has a certain value. In first grade, your child learned that "two" was the same as "2" and meant "two things." But by fourth grade, your child has developed a much more sophisticated idea of numbers, including the fact that place refers to the value of the digit, relative to its location in the number. The 4 in 45 is not the same as the 4 in 24, even though both digits are 4.

What Your Fourth Grader Should Be Learning

Your fourth grader should be able to locate numbers on a number line and understand that the number 42 means a number with 4 tens and 2 ones. By now, he should also understand that 42 can also be written as 2 tens and 22 ones. He probably knows all the ordinals (such as first, second, third).

He should be able to identify the place value for any given digit in a written number, and should be able to take numbers in word form and turn them into a number (so six thousand three hundred and forty five is written *6,345*).

What You and Your Child Can Do

Check your child's math homework and papers, and note whether there are any weak areas. Quite often, problems with math concepts are problems either with vocabulary or with the underlying math facts.

What Tests May Ask

Standardized tests may include questions in which students must order numbers from smallest to largest, or choose odd or even numbers. Students may have to write one numeral as an expanded numeral, or an expanded numeral as one number. Other questions may ask students to choose a number between two other numbers.

Practice Skill: Numeration

Directions: Choose the correct answer.

1   What whole number is one greater than 11?

(A)   9

(B)   12

(C)   8

(D)   10

2   Which of the following answers is the expanded numeral for 946?

(A)   9 + 4 + 6

(B)   90 + 40 + 6

(C)   900 + 40 + 6

(D)   900 + 40 + 60

3   How would you write 30,000 + 5,000 + 400 + 40 + 6?

(A)   35,446

(B)   350,446

(C)   30,546

(D)   35,046

4   Fill in the missing number: 30,630 = 30,000 + □ + 30

(A)   60

(B)   6

(C)   6,000

(D)   600

5 Complete the pattern: 9, 7, 5, 3, ☐

    Ⓐ 2

    Ⓑ 1

    Ⓒ 4

    Ⓓ 0

6 Which of these numbers is between 393,712 and 400,157?

    Ⓐ 188,712

    Ⓑ 400,158

    Ⓒ 399,813

    Ⓓ 393,217

(See page 97 for answer key.)

Number Concepts

Number concepts involve a knowledge of place value in great detail as well as more math vocabulary: even numbers, odd numbers, multiples, and prime numbers. Your child will also be analyzing number patterns by examining a series of numbers that share some relationship, which he must figure out. Then, he uses that rule to predict the next number in the pattern.

What Your Fourth Grader Should Be Learning

By fourth grade, your child will be expected to be able to identify number patterns and understand even, odd, or prime numbers (prime numbers are those numbers whose only factors are 1 and the number itself.) He should understand place value through the millions. The most difficult number concept involves analyzing number patterns. Here your child will examine a series of numbers that share some relationship. He must figure out the relationship or the rule, and then use that rule to predict the next number in the pattern.

What Tests May Ask

Most standardized tests will explore how well your child understands number concepts by presenting a list of numbers and asking students to choose the odd, even, or prime number from among the list. Tests will ask students to fill in missing numbers in a sequence, and ask a series of questions thoroughly exploring how well the student understands place value. In other attempts at assessing knowledge of place value, the test may present students with a series of figures in a certain pattern, and ask which one is missing from the pattern.

Practice Skill: Number Concepts

Directions: Choose the correct answer for the following questions.

7 Which of these numbers has a 5 in the hundreds place?

    Ⓐ 3150

    Ⓑ 5206

    Ⓒ 5352

    Ⓓ 4502

8 Sixty three thousand eighty =

Ⓐ 63,080

Ⓑ 63,808

Ⓒ 63,800

Ⓓ 63,008

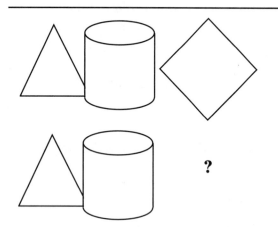

9 Which shape is missing from the above picture?

Ⓐ

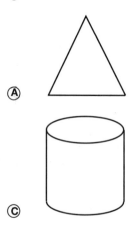

Ⓐ

Ⓒ

Ⓓ

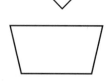

10 How many of these numbers are odd?

1 4 6 27 49 88

Ⓐ 1

Ⓑ 2

Ⓒ 3

Ⓓ 4

11 What does the 8 in 4283 mean?

Ⓐ 8

Ⓑ 8000

Ⓒ 80

Ⓓ 800

12 Karen was selling boxes of cookies to her friends. In her first week she sold 5, the next week she sold 9, and the third week she sold 13. If she keeps selling cookies in the same pattern, how many would she sell next week?

Ⓐ 15

Ⓑ 19

Ⓒ 10

Ⓓ 17

13 Which of these numbers is a prime number?

Ⓐ 4

Ⓑ 8

Ⓒ 3

Ⓓ 6

(See page 97 for answer key.)

Number Properties

Three types of skills are tested in the area of number properties:

- rounding or estimation,
- number sentences, and
- the order in solving a simple equation.

What Your Fourth Grader Should Be Learning

By the fourth grade, your child has been rounding numbers for quite some time; by now, he probably has heard all about number sentences (a simple equation that contains only numbers).

What You And Your Child Can Do

Estimation is such a natural skill that your child probably has a good idea of what to do. All you've got to do is let your child see you estimating, and have him join in. About how many hot dogs will we need to cook for the barbecue? About how long will it take for the marshmallows to melt for the S'mores? About how many twigs do we need to get ready for the bonfire? The more chances he has to estimate, the better an estimator he will be.

What Tests May Ask

Standardized tests in fourth grade will ask a variety of questions relating to number properties, including how to round a variety of numbers to the nearest ten, hundred, and so on. They will provide equations and ask students to fill in the missing number and ask a variety of number puzzle questions.

Practice Skill: Number Properties

Directions: Choose the correct answer for the following questions.

14 What is 569 rounded to the nearest ten?

- (A) 580
- (B) 570
- (C) 470
- (D) 670

15 Fill in the missing number: $\Box \times 9 = 63$

- (A) 13
- (B) 5
- (C) 6
- (D) 7

16 What symbol should go in the box in this equation: $3 \Box 12 = 36$?

- (A) +
- (B) −
- (C) ×
- (D) ÷

17 The sum of two numbers is 8. Their difference is two. What are the two numbers?

- (A) 4 and 2
- (B) 5 and 3
- (C) 1 and 7
- (D) 4 and 4

(See page 97 for answer key.)

Fractions and Decimals

Most children don't start out in first grade hating math, but many finish fourth grade avowed mathophobes—and often the study of fractions gets the blame.

Yet fractions needn't be that difficult to master, especially considering that your child uses fractions all the time. If he knows how to double the amount of hot fudge to go on his sundae to make enough for himself and a friend, he's using fractions. If he knows how much half a pizza is, or that 3/4 of a candy bar is more than 1/4, he's using fractions.

After spending most of the year on the basics of mathematics, near the end of fourth grade your child will probably be introduced to fractions: both adding and subtracting with like and unlike denominators. The hardest problem with this for most fourth graders is finding the lowest common denominator:

1. Find the lowest common denominator by systematically guessing.

2. Divide the old denominator into the lowest common denominator.

3. Multiply that number by the old numerator.

4. You get the new numerator.

If your child doesn't know his math facts very well, he won't learn how to add and subtract fractions as quickly as he could.

What Your Fourth Grader Should Be Learning

By the fourth grade, your child should know what decimals and fractions are, and be able to change fractions into decimals and decimals into fractions. He should be able to add and subtract fractions and decimals, rank fractions and decimals from smallest to largest, and find the least common denominator.

What Tests May Ask

Standardized tests of fractions and decimals will ask students to order fractions and decimals from smallest to largest; and to find the least common denominator. Tests may present a partially shaded figure and ask (in decimals) how much of the shape is colored in. They may ask for fractions' other names (as in "What's another name for 2/4?") and to identify place in a given decimal.

Practice Skill: Fractions

Directions: Choose the correct answer for the following questions.

18 $\frac{1}{5} + \frac{3}{5} =$

   Ⓐ 2/5

   Ⓑ 1/5

   Ⓒ 3/5

   Ⓓ 4/5

   Ⓔ none of these

19 $\frac{1}{3} + \frac{1}{3} =$

   Ⓐ 1/3

   Ⓑ 2/3

   Ⓒ 1/4

   Ⓓ 1/6

   Ⓔ none of these

20 $5\frac{1}{6}$
$+\ 2\frac{2}{6}$

Ⓐ $7\frac{1}{2}$

Ⓑ $8\frac{1}{2}$

Ⓒ $7\frac{4}{6}$

Ⓓ $6\frac{1}{6}$

Ⓔ none of these

---

21 $9/11 - 5/11 =$

Ⓐ 3/11

Ⓑ 7/11

Ⓒ 4/11

Ⓓ 1/2

Ⓔ none of these

---

22 $\frac{9}{10}$

$-\ \frac{4}{10}$

Ⓐ 6/10

Ⓑ 1/2

Ⓒ 3/10

Ⓓ 4/10

---

23 Which of these numbers falls between 4.79 and 4.97?

Ⓐ 4.98

Ⓑ 4.68

Ⓒ 4.83

Ⓓ 4.78

---

24 Which of the following choices is the same as $0.25?

Ⓐ five tenths of a dollar

Ⓑ one fourth of a dollar

Ⓒ two tenths of a dollar

Ⓓ two hundredths of a dollar

---

25 Which decimal is the same as five thousandths?

Ⓐ 0.05

Ⓑ 0.005

Ⓒ 0.0500

Ⓓ 0.050

---

26 Dacia and June watched a movie that lasted two and a half hours. What decimal shows how long the movie was?

Ⓐ 25 hours

Ⓑ 2.5 hours

Ⓒ 2.05 hours

Ⓓ 2.30 hours

---

27 Rank these decimals from least to greatest: 8.23, 8.95, 8.54, 8.10

Ⓐ 8.10, 8.54, 8.23, 8.95

Ⓑ 8.95, 8.54, 8.23, 8.10

Ⓒ 8.10, 8.23, 8.54, 8.95

Ⓓ 8.23, 8.10, 8.95, 8.54

28 Which of the decimals below is the smallest number?

    Ⓐ   2.03

    Ⓑ   2.19

    Ⓒ   2.90

    Ⓓ   2.13

(See pages 97–98 for answer key.)

CHAPTER 8

Math Computation

Success on the computation portion of a standardized test at the fourth-grade level depends on knowing math facts and understanding the processes of regrouping, operating with fractions, short division, and long division. The better your child can automatically recall her math facts for addition, subtraction, multiplication, and division, the better she will do on computation.

What Your Fourth Grader Should Be Learning

Fourth grade is an important bridge between the basic math skills that were taught in the early elementary grades and the more sophisticated ideas that will be introduced in fifth and sixth grades.

Your child should be able to add, subtract, multiply, and divide by several digits and with remainders (remembering the four steps of a long division problem), and should be confident with regrouping. She should be familiar with estimating and rounding off, with mental arithmetic, and with converting from one unit of measurement to another; she should also be starting to work with decimals and simple fractions.

What You and Your Child Can Do

Math in Action. Your child uses math all the time and never realizes it. Take every opportunity to point out the times when she's using "math in action!"

YOU: So, you want to take cookies to school to share with your class. How will you decide how many to take?

CHILD: Well, there are 30 children in my class.

YOU: So if each one got one cookie, how many cookies would you need?

CHILD: That's easy! 30.

YOU: How did you reach that conclusion?

CHILD: Well ... I just added.

YOU: Okay. Let's say you want each child to have 5 cookies. There are 30 children in the class. How would you figure that out?

CHILD: Well, I guess I could add...but that would take a long time. I could multiply 5 cookies times 30 kids. That would be 150 cookies!

YOU: Very good. Now, how many dozen would that be?

CHILD: I don't know!

YOU: Let's think about that. There are 12 cookies in one dozen, right?

CHILD: So you could divide 150 cookies by 12... That would be 12 dozen with 6 left over...

YOU: Can you say the remainder as a fraction?

CHILD: That would be...12 dozen and another half dozen. Twelve and a half dozen!

Mystery Operation. Give your child a word problem. Have her guess the operation.

YOU: Your friend got 10 candy canes at Christmas. She gave 5 to you. How many does she have left?

CHILD: Subtraction!

Multiplication War. Play the card game "War" with your child (remove face cards first) but instead of the traditional rules, each player throws a card and shouts out the product of the two cards. Whoever gives the correct answer first gets to keep the two cards.

Remainder Tips. Many fourth graders struggle with the idea of remainders—the notion that you can have such an untidy resolution to a math problem as a remainder can be hard for them to grasp. Put this in perspective by asking your child what would happen if she baked a dozen cupcakes but had only 10 guests at a party. Would she end up with everything coming out even, or would there be a remainder? Sometimes putting math into perspective using everyday examples can make things clearer.

What Tests May Ask

At the fourth-grade level, standardized tests include questions on adding columns of numbers and numbers with decimals; subtracting, multiplying, and dividing one- and two-digit numbers; adding and subtracting fractions, and naming the place value for numbers through millions.

Math Facts

Math facts should be old news for fourth graders, since they first heard this term in second grade, when they learned addition and subtraction facts up to 20. If your child is still counting on fingers or looking at her toes and counting in her head for the right answer, you

need to start immediately to refresh her memory on math facts. She should know them as well as she knows the multiplication tables, which means just about as well as she knows her own name.

You should start by testing her with all the addition and subtraction facts to 20, so you can find out which ones she knows, which are shaky, and which she doesn't know at all. Ask math facts while driving in the car, while waiting for the dentist, or while chopping vegetables in the kitchen. When she knows addition and subtraction through 20 thoroughly, move on to multiplication. Ask her to recite the tables, one by one. Any that she doesn't know must be repeated until they become automatic.

Math facts are important because they're the arithmetic building blocks—they pave the way for more complex mathematical exercises and they'll slow her down if she doesn't know them. A child who has to stop and count on her fingers will be at a real disadvantage—at school and on standardized tests—as she moves on into long division, fractions, algebra, and beyond.

Regrouping

Once your child knows the basic math facts, she can concentrate on the processes she'll need in fourth-grade math. The first multistep process to learn is regrouping (carrying and borrowing) in addition, subtraction, and multiplication problems.

Regrouping is usually introduced in second grade, but some children make errors because they don't align the numbers properly. (If this is your child's problem, have her copy the problems onto graph paper with each number in a separate box.) If your child's penmanship is so poor that she's making mistakes, go ahead and copy the problems for her out of the book. Neatness can be corrected farther down the road. What she needs to work on now is the process of doing the problem.

Addition

By fourth grade, adding should be second nature to your child. By the end of third grade, your child should have had an understanding of place value, addition of multidigit numbers, and regrouping. Make sure that your child has had lots of practice with two-digit regrouping, and that she can complete the procedure without hesitation. Once your child understands the concept, it can be applied to larger numbers. Regrouping is an important concept, so make sure your child fully understands it in relation to addition. In some schools, simple addition of fractions begins in third grade; other schools don't introduce this topic until near the end of fourth grade.

What Tests May Ask

In fourth grade, standardized tests include questions on adding multidigit numbers, dollars and cents, and fractions. Addition questions are presented in both single-line and double-line problems. Students should also expect to see problems such as this:

$$43 + \square = 53$$

Practice Skill: Addition

Directions: Choose the correct answer to each addition problem.

1.
```
   33
   44
 + 55
```
- (A) 132
- (B) 242
- (C) 119
- (D) 130
- (E) none of these

2.
```
   469
 + 12
```
- (A) 471
- (B) 481
- (C) 581
- (D) 571
- (E) none of these

3. $32 + 29 + 8 =$
- (A) 69
- (B) 59
- (C) 80
- (D) 68
- (E) none of these

4. $5326 + 1401 =$
- (A) 6227
- (B) 6277
- (C) 5617
- (D) 6727
- (E) none of these

5.
```
   $8.95
 +$3.19
```
- (A) $12.23
- (B) $12.14
- (C) $22.23
- (D) $22.03
- (E) none of these

(See page 98 for answer key.)

Subtraction

By fourth grade, your child should have a solid understanding of the basic subtraction facts and should comprehend that subtraction *starts with a larger group from which a part is taken away.* She should understand the concepts of place value, subtraction of multidigit numbers, and regrouping.

What Tests May Ask

Standardized tests for fourth graders include questions about subtracting decimals, subtracting in dollars and cents, and multidigit subtraction. There will also be questions on subtracting fractions, which will be written in two ways:

$$\frac{5}{11} - \frac{4}{11} \qquad \text{or} \qquad \begin{array}{r} \frac{5}{11} \\ - \frac{4}{11} \\ \hline \end{array}$$

Practice Skill: Subtraction

Directions: Choose the correct answer for the following problems.

6
$$\begin{array}{r} 3340 \\ - 1002 \\ \hline \end{array}$$

- Ⓐ 1228
- Ⓑ 2348
- Ⓒ 2338
- Ⓓ 2248
- Ⓔ none of these

7 4002 − 700 =

- Ⓐ 3302
- Ⓑ 4302
- Ⓒ 4402
- Ⓓ 3402
- Ⓔ none of the above

8
$$\begin{array}{r} 52.4 \\ - 1.5 \\ \hline \end{array}$$

- Ⓐ 51.9
- Ⓑ 40.9
- Ⓒ 40.8
- Ⓓ 41.9
- Ⓔ none of these

(See page 98 for answer key.)

Multiplication

Multiplication tables are usually presented in third grade, but that doesn't mean there isn't more to learn in fourth grade. In addition to continued drill on the multiplication facts, your child needs to understand that multiplication is simply the combination of sets of equal amounts, similar to repeated addition. Thus, you could solve 53 + 53 + 53 + 53 + 53, or you could multiply 53 × 5.

In fourth grade, your child's teacher will introduce multidigit multiplication, in which a two-digit number is first multiplied by a one-digit number:

$$\begin{array}{r} 24 \\ \times 2 \\ \hline \end{array}$$
2 digit number
multiplier

As with addition and subtraction, your child first learns the concept without having to carry across place values (as illustrated above). Once your child understands this, the teacher will introduce multiplication with carrying:

$$\begin{array}{r} 25 \\ \times\ 2 \\ \hline \end{array}$$

What Tests May Ask

Fourth-grade standardized tests present multiplication questions in a range of formats, from the very simple (multiplying one digit by two digits) to the fairly complex (multiplying two digits by two digits, decimals, and fractions). In addition, your child should be prepared not only to select the correct answer from among a number of wrong ones, but to realize the possibility that the correct answer might not be listed at all. This makes guessing more difficult.

Practice Skill: Multiplication

Directions: Choose the correct answer for the following problems.

9 $\begin{array}{r} 40 \\ \times\ 4 \\ \hline \end{array}$

   Ⓐ 180

   Ⓑ 160

   Ⓒ 164

   Ⓓ 184

   Ⓔ none of these

10 $1000 \times 5 =$

   Ⓐ 500

   Ⓑ 50,000

   Ⓒ 5,000

   Ⓓ 500,000

   Ⓔ none of these

11 $5 \times 11 = \square$

   Ⓐ 54

   Ⓑ 5

   Ⓒ 55

   Ⓓ 66

   Ⓔ none of these

12 $203 \times 8 =$

   Ⓐ 1624

   Ⓑ 1623

   Ⓒ 1632

   Ⓓ 2653

   Ⓔ none of these

(See page 98 for answer key.)

Division

Long and short division are important skills that are usually first introduced in the fourth-grade curriculum after the children seem comfortable with multiplication. Division is the reverse of multiplication, just as subtraction is the reverse of addition.

While short division is a fairly simple concept that can be understood as the opposite of multiplication, long division is often quite complicated and challenging for fourth graders to master.

Your child needs to remember the steps in long division:

1. Divide.
2. Multiply.
3. Subtract.
4. Bring Down.

If your child has trouble remembering the steps, try using a mnemonic to help her remember the steps in order: Dad, Mom, Sister, Brother is the classic. Or let your child make up her own mnemonic using the same letters, D, M, S, and B: Don't Make Silly Boo-boos. Dogs May Slurp Beans.

With the help of a mnemonic and math facts memorized perfectly, your child needs to practice until the process is well-learned. By the end of fourth grade, your child should understand the concept of division and be able to recognize the symbols used to denote division. Recognizing that division is the reverse of multiplication will make the process easier to understand.

What Tests May Ask

Standardized tests in fourth grade present questions in both short division and long division with remainders, using both division symbols. Students will be asked to choose the correct answer from a group of possibilities, including "none of these."

Practice Skill: Division

Directions: Choose the correct answer for the following problems.

13 $538 \div 3 =$

Ⓐ 178 R2

Ⓑ 168 R3

Ⓒ 179 R3

Ⓓ 180

Ⓔ none of these

14 $45 \div 5 =$

Ⓐ 8

Ⓑ 7

Ⓒ 9

Ⓓ 6

Ⓔ none of these

15 $15 \div 3 = \square$

Ⓐ 6

Ⓑ 8

Ⓒ 4

Ⓓ 5

Ⓔ none of these

16 $25 \div \square = 5$

Ⓐ 5

Ⓑ 7

Ⓒ 6

Ⓓ 4

Ⓔ none of these

(See page 98 for answer key.)

CHAPTER 9

Math Applications

Math applications is that part of mathematics that involves using math in real, everyday situations. Both in the classroom and on standardized tests, students in fourth grade spend a lot of time learning how to apply mathematics; estimating weight and size; reading a calendar and thermometer; recognizing plane and solid figures; understanding bar graphs, tables, and charts; finding perimeters and areas; solving word problems; understanding time; and recognizing the value of money.

What Your Fourth Grader Should Be Learning

Fourth graders should have a working knowledge of basic math facts, geometry, measurement, and word problem solving. They should be able to tell time, understand money and make change easily, and understand both metric and nonmetric units of measure.

What Tests May Ask

On the major standardized tests, three main areas are tested in the section known as math applications:

- geometry,
- measurement, and
- problem solving.

In addition, a solid knowledge of math facts and vocabulary is essential when taking any of these tests.

Test items in math applications usually include word problems composed of several sentences with math vocabulary, so it's vital that your child know these basic terms (such as the definitions of "perimeter" or "area") or his answers will be wrong (even if he knows how to multiply length by width). At the same time, if your child knows exactly how to find the area of a square but he doesn't know his math facts well enough to do the computations, his knowledge won't help him much on the tests.

What You and Your Child Can Do

Despite the number of mathophobes in the world, it's quite possible to have a lot of fun with math at home, while building your child's confidence that indeed, he can do math. Here are some ways you can make math enjoyable and reinforce skills at the same time:

Play Games. You'd be amazed at how many games can enhance your child's mathematical ability—not just in straight computation (such as adding two dice together), but in strategy and problem solving as well. For example, in the game of Sorry, one of the possible moves is a "7" that you can split between two of your four pieces, so that one piece moves 1 space and the other moves 6, or one moves 4 and the other 3, and so on. It takes strategy and good math skills to figure out how to break down that move for the best outcome.

Monopoly. There's nothing like a good (long!) game of Monopoly for teaching money. Make your child banker and see how quickly he'll master making change, buying and selling properties, and charging rent!

Computer Games. Educational games designed for computers can be fun and extremely helpful when it comes to learning math skills. A host of games are especially designed to teach math in such fun ways that your child probably won't even realize it's mathematics. *Math Blaster* and *Treasure Mountain* are just two of the many possibilities.

Jr. Julia Child. If you can stand a bit of mess, letting your fourth grader loose in your kitchen can be a valuable lesson in measurement and math—and there's a real reward at the end, if you let him concoct a tasty cake or delicious homemade ice cream. Measuring, dividing (if you need to halve a recipe), and multiplying (for doubling recipes) units of measure and problem solving are all common occurrences in the kitchen.

Mr. Wizard. A fun way to teach thermometer reading is to set up a little weather station in your backyard. You can buy the supplies at your local educational toy store or teacher supply store. Start with a simple thermometer, a rain gauge, and perhaps a barometer. Have your child take the readings every morning and log his findings on a monthly chart. See if he can correlate his measurements with weather changes.

Geometry

Geometry: Odds are, when you were in school, you either loved it or hated it. Some parents find that a previously math-phobic child loves geometry; others find that a budding Einstein suddenly can't bear mathematics when it comes

time to break out the cones and cubes. Experts aren't sure why, but geometry seems to activate fundamentally different parts of the brain and to require very specific skills. In the fourth grade, geometry study includes learning about all sorts of figures, learning about lines and their properties, and learning how to find perimeters and areas.

What Your Fourth Grader Should Be Learning

Your child should be aware of the basics of geometry and be able to find the perimeter and area of regular shapes like squares and rectangles. He should know how to find area, perimeter, circumference, diameter, and radius.

Moreover, if your child is going to spend some time in geometry country, he's got to learn the lingo to do well. He should be familiar with all these terms, which he will need to know to do well on a standardized test:

- acute, obtuse, and right angles;
- perpendicular lines;
- parallelograms;
- parallel lines;
- equilateral and right triangles; and
- solid figures including sphere, cylinder, pyramid, cone, and rectangular prism.

What Tests May Ask

Standardized tests ask students to identify certain shapes, give definitions of geometric terms, and select the matching shape. They may ask questions about how to find perimeters and areas of figures. Questions will ask students to find the one correct answer in a group of incorrect ones, and to choose the incorrect response in a list of correct answers. There is usually a "none of the above" choice as well.

What You and Your Child Can Do

Shape Safari. Here's a good game to play when your child has a friend to stay: Give both children a list of geometric shapes (circle, square, rectangle, oval, triangle, polygon), together with a pad and pencil. Have them write down as many of the shapes as they can find by looking around the house: the door is a rectangle, the window is a square, the cat's head is a circle and its ears are triangles, and so on. What shape was the hardest to find? What was the most common?

Try finding shapes as you are driving down the highway. Don't just stick with the easy ones, like squares and circles. Go for the rectangular prism, the pyramid, the ray, and the line segment. Look for lines that are parallel and perpendicular. Most geometry questions can be answered if the child at this age knows what the terms mean.

Visual Memory. Have your child sketch a picture of a pencil and eraser, his foot, and his stapler from memory. (The better the visual memory, the easier geometry will be.) Now have him compare the actual article with his drawing. Which drawing was best?

Toothpick Fun. Keep a plastic bag of a few toothpicks with you in your purse or pocket. When you have some down time (in a restaurant, waiting for an appointment, or in the car), ask your child to make four shapes with the toothpicks; see how many enclosed shapes he can make. If more than one child is with you, stage a competition to see who can make the most shapes in 30 seconds.

Make a Geoboard. Let your child hammer 16 nails into a block of wood in a square pattern, four nails long by four nails wide. Include a rubber band, and have him practice making different shapes.

Practice Skill: Geometry

Directions: Choose the correct answer for the following questions.

1   A jar is shaped most like a:

   Ⓐ   cube

   Ⓑ   cylinder

   Ⓒ   rectangular prism

   Ⓓ   sphere

---

2   What is the area of this shape? (Area = length x width)

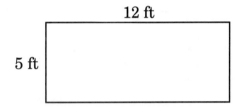

   Ⓐ   50 feet

   Ⓑ   60 feet

   Ⓒ   60 inches

   Ⓓ   120 feet

---

3   What angles are in this figure?

   Ⓐ   right angles

   Ⓑ   acute angles

   Ⓒ   obtuse angles

   Ⓓ   no angles

---

4 Which of the following shapes is NOT a polygon?

Ⓐ

Ⓑ

Ⓒ

Ⓓ

5 How many faces does the figure below have?

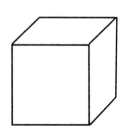

Ⓐ 3

Ⓑ 6

Ⓒ 4

Ⓓ 5

6 _____

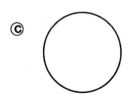

Line segments like the ones above that stay the same distance apart from each other are called:

Ⓐ intersecting

Ⓑ perpendicular

Ⓒ parallel

Ⓓ rays

7 The figure below is called a:

⟶

Ⓐ parallel line

Ⓑ ray

Ⓒ line segment

Ⓓ line

(See page 98 for answer key.)

Measurement

Measurement includes more than just knowing the details of inches or feet; it also involves understanding time, temperature, calendars, and money.

What Your Fourth Grader Should Be Learning

By fourth grade, children are expected to be able to measure using units of time, money, temperature, volume, length, and width; should understand both metric units and inches, feet, miles, gallons, and so on; and should be able to quickly combine coins and count out different amounts: one quarter, one nickel, and three pennies.

What Tests May Ask

Standardized tests present clocks, calendars, rulers, and thermometers and ask questions about measurements to determine how well children know their measurement facts. Questions will include both those that exclude (which shape does NOT belong) and those that ask your child to choose the correct answer from among several wrong ones.

What You and Your Child Can Do

Helping your child to become better at measurement is an easy chore around the house, because it's such a practical skill. You can measure distances and lengths using real objects, at home or in the car. Just be sure you have a traditional ruler, yardstick, or tape measure, as well as a measuring device that shows metric units.

Guesstimate. Ask your children to estimate: How high do you think that house is? How far do you estimate it is around this track?

Conversion. Let your child practice converting between measures: feet to yards, meters to centimeters. Children usually enjoy measurement because it's concrete and novel.

Kitchen Scavengers. Do volume measurements in the kitchen: gallons, cups, pints, and quarts. Send your child on a scavenger hunt for measuring words in the pantry and he will soon notice metric units as well as quarts and pounds. This is a good ending math activity after your child has recited his 8 times table while you are cooking supper: "Now find some way I could pour out a pint of apple juice. Find me something that is measured in ounces."

Taking a Temperature. When reviewing temperature, let your child use your digital thermometer to measure the temperatures of ice water, a cup of tea, or his own body temperature. Children love to conduct little experiments like this, and your child will be getting practice reading a scale. Be sure to point out Fahrenheit and Celsius.

Fun Money. Money skills are best taught in real, everyday situations. By now your child should also be able to make change for amounts over one dollar, so be sure to let him practice in the store. Have him figure out how much change he should get, and then verify it at the cash register.

I Spy. Get tough with this game now, and try the following questions:

- I spy something between an inch and four inches long.
- I spy something that weighs about as much as our car.
- I spy something that weighs as little as a feather.
- I spy something that can hold about an ounce of birdseed.
- I spy something that could hold about a cup of liquid.

Measurement Hunt. This one works well if your fourth grader has a friend over for the night. Make up two lists and send them each off looking for:

- an object less than an inch long,
- something bigger than a breadbox,
- something with a circumference bigger than five inches, and
- something that weighs about a pound.

Practice Skill: Measurement

Directions: Choose the correct answer for the following questions.

8 A trout is about 30 inches long. A large American lobster is about two feet long. Which is longer, the trout or the lobster?

   (A) lobster

   (B) trout

   (C) They are both the same.

   (D) Don't have enough information to tell.

9 12 yd. = _____ feet

    Ⓐ   35 feet

    Ⓑ   36 feet

    Ⓒ   3 feet

    Ⓓ   30 feet

    Ⓔ   none of the above

10 Sarah buys two Pokemon videos. Each one costs $19.95, including tax. She gives the clerk two $20 bills. How much change will Sarah get?

    Ⓐ $0.25

    Ⓑ $1.10

    Ⓒ $0.10

    Ⓓ $0.50

    Ⓔ   none of the above

11 How many quart containers of water does it take to fill a five-gallon aquarium?

    Ⓐ   10 quarts

    Ⓑ   15 quarts

    Ⓒ   5 quarts

    Ⓓ   20 quarts

    Ⓔ   none of the above

12 How many ounces are there in a five-pound box of sugar?

    Ⓐ   50

    Ⓑ   80

    Ⓒ   70

    Ⓓ   60

    Ⓔ   none of the above

13 If 1,000 milliliters (mL) equals 1 liter (L), how many 1-mL eyedroppers would it take to fill a 2-liter bottle with water?

    Ⓐ   1,000 eyedroppers

    Ⓑ   200 eyedroppers

    Ⓒ   20,000 eyedroppers

    Ⓓ   2,000 eyedroppers

    Ⓔ   none of the above

14 Brittany ate breakfast and got dressed in 30 minutes. She watched TV for an hour and 15 minutes, read a magazine for 15 minutes, and worked on the computer for 30 minutes. After that, she went outside and played with her friends. If she started eating breakfast at 7:30 a.m., what time did she go outside?

    Ⓐ   10 a.m.

    Ⓑ   9 a.m.

    Ⓒ   9:30 a.m.

    Ⓓ   10:30 a.m.

    Ⓔ   none of the above

15 The length of the paper clip is:

    Ⓐ   2 inches

    Ⓑ   ½ inch

    Ⓒ   2½ inch

    Ⓓ   1 inch

16 Choose the best estimate of the height of a classmate.

Ⓐ 40 feet

Ⓑ 4 inches

Ⓒ 45 yards

Ⓓ 50 inches

17 Choose the best estimate of the depth of the middle of the ocean.

Ⓐ 10 inches

Ⓑ 4 feet

Ⓒ 2½ feet

Ⓓ 6 miles

18 Which of these measures is the largest?

Ⓐ 3 gallons

Ⓑ 8 cups

Ⓒ 5 quarts

Ⓓ 1 ounce

19 Which of these would best be measured in centimeters?

Ⓐ a football field

Ⓑ a football

Ⓒ a speck of dirt on the football field

Ⓓ a helmet

20 Which of the following coin combinations does NOT equal $1.00?

Ⓐ 10 dimes

Ⓑ 40 nickels

Ⓒ 4 quarters

Ⓓ 100 pennies

21 What is the correct time as shown on the clock above?

Ⓐ 4:05

Ⓑ 4:00

Ⓒ 1:25

Ⓓ 5:05

(See page 98 for answer key.)

Problem Solving

After your child has mastered completing math facts quickly and accurately, math vocabulary, and multistep processes like long division, and converting fractions and decimals, it's time to put all these pieces together in order to solve a problem. If any of the earlier concepts are weak, your child will have a harder time solving problems, because it's more likely he'll make careless mistakes.

What Your Fourth Grader Should Be Learning

In fourth grade, your child should be able to read a word problem of several sentences and should be able to identify the information embedded in the problem. He should be able to state clearly what information the problem is asking for and ignore information not needed to solve the problem.

What You and Your Child Can Do

If your child is struggling with word problems (and that's not unusual at this age, when the right parietal lobe of the brain, which governs logic, is still developing), ask him to do the problem aloud as you watch. This will help you figure out what the problem is. It may be a vocabulary problem, a wrong math fact, or just not enough practice on a math process.

On the other hand, many children in fourth grade seem to read a word problem and then stop, bewildered and uncertain what to do next. If this is your child's problem, you can teach your child a logical way to approach even the trickiest math challenges, which may be all your child needs. Here's what to tell your child:

1. Read the problem out loud.

2. Identify all the given facts, in order.

3. Clearly state what the question is asking.

Here's an example:

A carton of writing paper has 10 packages of paper in it and sells for $30. You can also buy the paper in individual packages for $4 per package. You have $40 to buy paper, which you're going to use to send out party invitations. The paper comes in blue and white. What would you buy?

YOU: List all the facts in this problem in order. State each fact in its own sentence.

CHILD: Okay. A carton of paper has 10 packages. It sells for $30. You can buy paper in individual packages. Individual packages cost $4 per package. I have $40 to buy paper. I'm going to use paper to send out invitations. The paper comes in blue and white. Which paper is the best buy? How many packages can you get for $40?

YOU: Good job! You got all the facts right. Now tell me one more thing.

CHILD: Which paper is the best buy?

YOU: Do they just want to know the total cost of paper? Or are they asking you to compare prices?

CHILD: Let's see...I'm not sure. I guess it would be too easy to just give a total, huh? It must be they want me to compare prices.

YOU: That's right. What do you have to do first to see which kind of paper is cheaper?

CHILD: Well, you would have to find out how much each pack of paper costs, and then compare them.

YOU: That's right. How would you find out how much one package of paper sold by the carton would cost?

CHILD: Divide the total cost of the carton by the number of packages. It would be...$3 each.

YOU: Right. And do you already know the cost of the individual package of paper sold by itself?

CHILD: Yes. It's $4.

YOU: So, you can see then...

CHILD: The paper sold by the carton is $1 cheaper a package!

YOU: Right. And how many cartons could you get?

CHILD: Well, one carton is $30. I'd have $10 left over, so I could get another three packages out of the carton with some change!

You can see that by logically talking through the problem, you can help your child to first identify the question being asked and then figure out how to answer it. You're teaching problem solving. But there is a second part of the experience you're not teaching. In this sort of problem, you have to set up the logical steps and then sit and wait while your child works it out in his mind.

It's very important to have the patience to lead your child up to this moment of awareness, then sit quietly and let your child think without being nudged or interrupted. If he doesn't make the connection, be patient. You may need to be more concrete; try drawing a picture of the packages of paper. Then let your child think again. Don't expect your child to catch on right away. Problem solving is not an easy skill for many fourth graders to master. Provide plenty of chances to practice.

Practice Skill: Problem Solving

Directions: Choose the correct answer for the following questions.

22 Mrs. Helvetica keeps 120 books in a large bookcase. Each large shelf holds 20 books. How many shelves are there in the bookcase?

- (A) 8
- (B) 6
- (C) 7
- (D) 9
- (E) none of these

23 Tom grew fruit to sell. There are 12 rutabagas for $0.40 each and 15 cantaloupes for $1.75 each. If he sells all his fruit, how much money will he have?

- (A) $31.05
- (B) $32.10
- (C) $41.05
- (D) $31.15
- (E) none of the above

24 Sandy scored 12 baskets for her team. Three of the baskets are worth 3 points, and the rest are worth 2 points. How many more 3-point baskets does she need in order to score 30 points?

- (A) 2
- (B) 3
- (C) 1
- (D) 0
- (E) none of the above

25 Hope and Anna's family is going to the beach. The motel costs $1,000 and they are staying 10 nights. How much does the motel cost for each night?

- (A) $250
- (B) $150
- (C) $90
- (D) $100
- (E) none of the above

26   In three days, Ms. Unruly drove 350
     miles, 205 miles, and 180 miles. What is
     the average number of miles that she
     drove each day?

Ⓐ   235

Ⓑ   240

Ⓒ   145

Ⓓ   345

Ⓔ   none of the above

(See page 98 for answer key.)

Web Sites and Resources for More Information

Homework

Homework Central
http://www.HomeworkCentral.com
Terrific site for students, parents, and teachers, filled with information, projects, and more.

Win the Homework Wars
(Sylvan Learning Centers)
http://www.educate.com/online/qa_peters.html

Reading and Grammar Help

Born to Read: How to Raise a Reader
http://www.ala.org/alsc/raise_a_reader.html

Guide to Grammar and Writing
http://webster.commnet.edu/hp/pages/darling/grammar.htm
Help with "plague words and phrases," grammar FAQs, sentence parts, punctuation, rules for common usage.

Internet Public Library: Reading Zone
http://www.ipl.org/cgi-bin/youth/youth.out

Keeping Kids Reading and Writing
http://www.tiac.net/users/maryl/

U.S. Dept. of Education: Helping Your Child Learn to Read
http://www.ed.gov/pubs/parents/Reading/index.html

Math Help

Center for Advancement of Learning
http://www.muskingum.edu/%7Ecal/database/Math2.html
Substitution and memory strategies for math.

Center for Advancement of Learning
http://www.muskingum.edu/%7Ecal/database/Math1.html
General tips and suggestions.

Math.com
http://www.math.com
The world of math online.

Math.com
http://www.math.com/student/testprep.html
Get ready for standardized tests.

Math.com: Homework Help in Math
http://www.math.com/students/homework.html

Math.com: Math for Homeschoolers
http://www.math.com/parents/homeschool.html

The Math Forum: Problems and Puzzles
http://forum.swarthmore.edu/library/resource_types/problems_puzzles
Lots of fun math puzzles and problems for grades K through 12.

The Math Forum: Math Tips and Tricks
http://forum.swarthmore.edu/k12/mathtips/mathtips.html

Tips on Testing

Books on Test Preparation

http://www.testbooksonline.com/preHS.asp
This site provides printed resources for parents who wish to help their children prepare for standardized school tests.

Core Knowledge Web Site

http://www.coreknowledge.org/
Site dedicated to providing resources for parents; based on the books of E. D. Hirsch, Jr., who wrote the *What Your X Grader Needs to Know* series.

Family Education Network

http://www.familyeducation.com/article/0,1120,
1-6219,00.html
This report presents some of the arguments against current standardized testing practices in the public schools. The site also provides links to family activities that help kids learn.

Math.com

http://www.math.com/students/testprep.html
Get ready for standardized tests.

Standardized Tests

http://arc.missouri.edu/k12/
K through 12 assessment tools and know-how.

Parents: Testing in Schools

KidSource: Talking to Your Child's Teacher about Standardized Tests

http://www.kidsource.com/kidsource/content2/
talking.assessment.k12.4.html
This site provides basic information to help parents understand their children's test results and provides pointers for how to discuss the results with their children's teachers.

eSCORE.com: State Test and Education Standards

http://www.eSCORE.com
Find out if your child meets the necessary requirements for your local schools. A Web site with experts from Brazelton Institute and Harvard's Project Zero.

Overview of States' Assessment Programs

http://ericae.net/faqs/

Parent Soup
Education Central: Standardized Tests

http://www.parentsoup.com/edcentral/testing
A parent's guide to standardized testing in the schools, written from a parent advocacy standpoint.

National Center for Fair and Open Testing, Inc. (FairTest)

342 Broadway
Cambridge, MA 02139
(617) 864-4810
http://www.fairtest.org

National Parent Information Network

http://npin.org

Publications for Parents from the U.S. Department of Education

http://www.ed.gov/pubs/parents/
An ever-changing list of information for parents available from the U.S. Department of Education.

State of the States Report

http://www.edweek.org/sreports/qc99/states/
indicators/in-intro.htm
A report on testing and achievement in the 50 states.

Testing: General Information

Academic Center for Excellence

http://www.acekids.com

American Association for Higher Education Assessment

http://www.aahe.org/assessment/web.htm

American Educational Research Association (AERA)

http://aera.net
An excellent link to reports on American education, including reports on the controversy over standardized testing.

American Federation of Teachers

555 New Jersey Avenue, NW
Washington, D.C. 20011

Association of Test Publishers Member Products and Services
http://www.testpublishers.org/memserv.htm

Education Week on the Web
http://www.edweek.org

ERIC Clearinghouse on Assessment and Evaluation
1131 Shriver Lab
University of Maryland
College Park, MD 20742
http://ericae.net
A clearinghouse of information on assessment and education reform.

FairTest: The National Center for Fair and Open Testing
http://fairtest.org/facts/ntfact.htm
http://fairtest.org/
The National Center for Fair and Open Testing is an advocacy organization working to end the abuses, misuses, and flaws of standardized testing and to ensure that evaluation of students and workers is fair, open, and educationally sound. This site provides many links to fact sheets, opinion papers, and other sources of information about testing.

National Congress of Parents and Teachers
700 North Rush Street
Chicago, Illinois 60611

National Education Association
1201 16th Street, NW
Washington, DC 20036

National School Boards Association
http://www.nsba.org
A good source for information on all aspects of public education, including standardized testing.

Testing Our Children: A Report Card on State Assessment Systems
http://www.fairtest.org/states/survey.htm
Report of testing practices of the states, with graphical links to the states and a critique of fair testing practices in each state.

Trends in Statewide Student Assessment Programs: A Graphical Summary
http://www.ccsso.org/survey96.html
Results of annual survey of states' departments of public instruction regarding their testing practices.

U.S. Department of Education
http://www.ed.gov/

Web Links for Parents Who Want to Help Their Children Achieve
http://www.liveandlearn.com/learn.html
This page offers many Web links to free and for-sale information and materials for parents who want to help their children do well in school. Titles include such free offerings as the Online Colors Game and questionnaires to determine whether your child is ready for school.

What Should Parents Know about Standardized Testing in the Schools?
http://www.rusd.k12.ca.us/parents/standard.html
An online brochure about standardized testing in the schools, with advice regarding how to become an effective advocate for your child.

Test Publishers Online

ACT: Information for Life's Transitions
http://www.act.org

American Guidance Service, Inc.
http://www.agsnet.com

Ballard & Tighe Publishers
http://www.ballard-tighe.com

Consulting Psychologists Press
http://www.cpp-db.com

CTB McGraw-Hill
http://www.ctb.com

Educational Records Bureau
http://www.erbtest.org/index.html

Educational Testing Service
http://www.ets.org

General Educational Development (GED) Testing Service
http://www.acenet.edu/calec/ged/home.html

Harcourt Brace Educational Measurement
http://www.hbem.com

Piney Mountain Press—A Cyber-Center for Career and Applied Learning
http://www.pineymountain.com

ProEd Publishing
http://www.proedinc.com

Riverside Publishing Company
http://www.hmco.com/hmco/riverside

Stoelting Co.
http://www.stoeltingco.com

Sylvan Learning Systems, Inc.
http://www.educate.com

Touchstone Applied Science Associates, Inc. (TASA)
http://www.tasa.com

Tests Online

(*Note:* We don't endorse tests; some may not have technical documentation. Evaluate the quality of any testing program before making decisions based on its use.)

Edutest, Inc.
http://www.edutest.com
Edutest is an Internet-accessible testing service that offers criterion-referenced tests for elementary school students, based upon the standards for K through 12 learning and achievement in the states of Virginia, California, and Florida.

Virtual Knowledge
http://www.smarterkids.com
This commercial service, which enjoys a formal partnership with Sylvan Learning Centers, offers a line of skills assessments for preschool through grade 9 for use in the classroom or the home. For free online sample tests, see the Virtual Test Center.

Read More about It

Abbamont, Gary W. *Test Smart: Ready-to-Use Test-Taking Strategies and Activities for Grades 5–12. Upper Saddle River,* NJ: Prentice Hall Direct, 1997.

Cookson, Peter W., and Joshua Halberstam. *A Parent's Guide to Standardized Tests in School: How to Improve Your Child's Chances for Success.* New York: Learning Express, 1998.

Frank, Steven, and Stephen Frank. *Test-Taking Secrets: Study Better, Test Smarter, and Get Great Grades (The Backpack Study Series).* Holbrook, MA: Adams Media Corporation, 1998.

Gilbert, Sara Dulaney. *How to Do Your Best on Tests: A Survival Guide.* New York: Beech Tree Books, 1998.

Gruber, Gary. *Dr. Gary Gruber's Essential Guide to Test-Taking for Kids, Grades 3–5.* New York: William Morrow & Co., 1986.

——. *Gary Gruber's Essential Guide to Test-Taking for Kids, Grades 6, 7, 8, 9.* New York: William Morrow & Co., 1997.

Leonhardt, Mary. *99 Ways to Get Kids to Love Reading and 100 Books They'll Love.* New York: Crown, 1997.

——. *Parents Who Love Reading, Kids Who Don't: How It Happens and What You Can Do about It.* New York: Crown, 1995.

McGrath, Barbara B. *The Baseball Counting Book.* Watertown, MA: Charlesbridge, 1999.

——. *More M&M's Brand Chocolate Candies Math.* Watertown, MA: Charlesbridge, 1998.

Mokros, Janice R. *Beyond Facts & Flashcards: Exploring Math with Your Kids.* Portsmouth, NH: Heinemann, 1996.

Romain, Trevor, and Elizabeth Verdick. *True or False?: Tests Stink!* Minneapolis: Free Spirit Publishing Co., 1999.

Schartz, Eugene M. *How to Double Your Child's Grades in School: Build Brilliance and Leadership into Your Child—from Kindergarten to College—in Just 5 Minutes a Day.* New York: Barnes & Noble, 1999.

Taylor, Kathe, and Sherry Walton. *Children at the Center: A Workshop Approach to Standardized Test Preparation, K–8.* Portsmouth, NH: Heinemann, 1998.

Tobia, Sheila. *Overcoming Math Anxiety.* New York: W. W. Norton & Company, Inc., 1995.

Tufariello, Ann Hunt. *Up Your Grades: Proven Strategies for Academic Success.* Lincolnwood, IL: VGM Career Horizons, 1996.

Vorderman, Carol. *How Math Works.* Pleasantville, NY: Reader's Digest Association, Inc., 1996.

Zahler, Kathy A. *50 Simple Things You Can Do to Raise a Child Who Loves to Read.* New York: IDG Books, 1997.

What Your Child's Test Scores Mean

Several weeks or months after your child has taken standardized tests, you will receive a report such as the TerraNova Home Report found in Figures 1 and 2. You will receive similar reports if your child has taken other tests. We briefly examine what information the reports include.

Look at the first page of the Home Report. Note that the chart provides labeled bars showing the child's performance. Each bar is labeled with the child's National Percentile for that skill area. When you know how to interpret them, national percentiles can be the most useful scores you encounter on reports such as this. Even when you are confronted with different tests that use different scale scores, you can always interpret percentiles the same way, regardless of the test. A percentile tells the percent of students who score at or below that level. A percentile of 25, for example, means that 25 percent of children taking the test scored at or below that score. (It also means that 75 percent of students scored above that score.) Note that the average is always at the 50th percentile.

On the right side of the graph on the first page of the report, the publisher has designated the ranges of scores that constitute average, above average, and below average. You can also use this slightly more precise key for interpreting percentiles:

PERCENTILE RANGE	LEVEL
2 and Below	Deficient
3–8	Borderline
9–23	Low Average
24–75	Average
76–97	High Average
98 and Up	Superior

The second page of the Home report provides a listing of the child's strengths and weaknesses, along with keys for mastery, partial mastery, and non-mastery of the skills. Scoring services determine these breakdowns based on the child's scores as compared with those from the national norm group.

Your child's teacher or guidance counselor will probably also receive a profile report similar to the TerraNova Individual Profile Report, shown in Figures 3 and 4. That report will be kept in your child's permanent record. The first aspect of this report to notice is that the scores are expressed both numerically and graphically.

First look at the score bands under National Percentile. Note that the scores are expressed as bands, with the actual score represented by a dot within each band. The reason we express the scores as bands is to provide an idea of the amount by which typical scores may vary for each student. That is, each band represents a

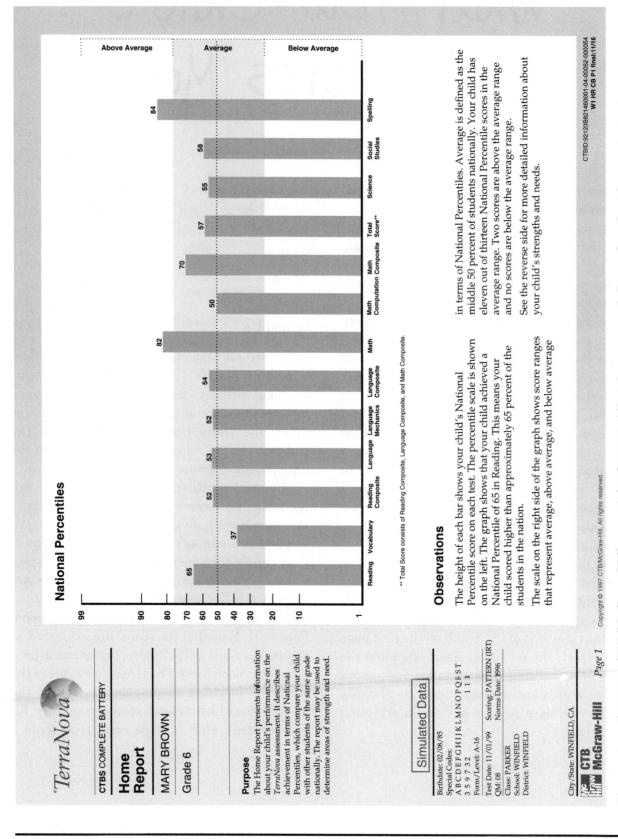

Figure 1 (Source: CTB/McGraw-Hill, copyright © 1997. All rights reserved. Reproduced with permission.)

TerraNova

CTBS COMPLETE BATTERY

Home Report

MARY BROWN

Grade 6

Purpose

This page of the Home Report presents information about your child's strengths and needs. This information is provided to help you monitor your child's academic growth.

Birthdate: 02/08/85
Special Codes:
A B C D E F G H I J K L M N O P Q R S T
3 5 9 7 3 2   1 1 1
Form/Level: A-16

Test Date: 11/01/99   Scoring: PATTERN (IRT)
QM: 08   Norms Date: 1996

Class: PARKER
School: WINFIELD
District: WINFIELD

City/State: WINFIELD, CA

CTB
McGraw-Hill   *Page 2*

Strengths

Reading
● Basic Understanding
● Analyze Text

Vocabulary
● Word Meaning
● Words in Context

Language
● Editing Skills
● Sentence Structure

Language Mechanics
● Sentences, Phrases, Clauses

Mathematics
● Computation and Numerical Estimation
● Operation Concepts

Mathematics Computation
● Add Whole Numbers
● Multiply Whole Numbers

Science
● Life Science
● Inquiry Skills

Social Studies
● Geographic Perspectives
● Economic Perspectives

Spelling
● Vowels
● Consonants

Key ● Mastery

General Interpretation

The left column shows your child's best areas of performance. In each case, your child has reached mastery level. The column at the right shows the areas within each test section where your child's scores are the lowest. In these cases, your child has not reached mastery level, although he or she may have reached partial mastery.

Needs

Reading
◐ Evaluate and Extend Meaning
○ Identify Reading Strategies

Vocabulary
○ Multimeaning Words

Language
◐ Writing Strategies

Language Mechanics
○ Writing Conventions

Mathematics
◐ Measurement
◐ Geometry and Spatial Sense

Mathematics Computation
○ Percents

Science
○ Earth and Space Science

Social Studies
◐ Historical and Cultural Perspectives

Spelling
No area of needs were identified for this content area

Key ◐ Partial Mastery   ○ **Non-Mastery**

Figure 2   (SOURCE: CTB/McGraw-Hill, copyright © 1997. All rights reserved. Reproduced with permission.)

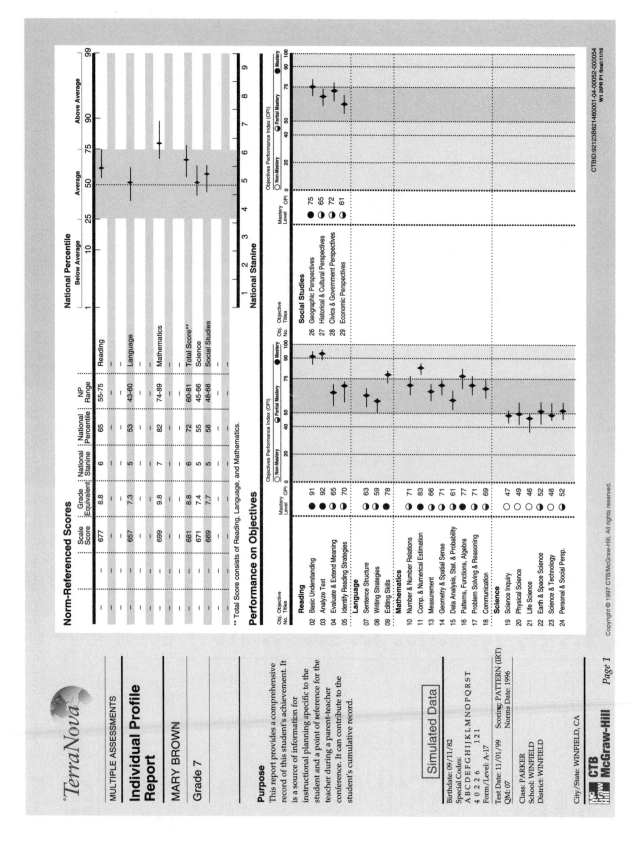

Figure 3 (SOURCE: CTB/McGraw-Hill, copyright © 1997. All rights reserved. Reproduced with permission.)

Observations

Norm-Referenced Scores

The top section of the report presents information about this student's achievement in several different ways. The National Percentile (NP) data and graph indicate how this student performed compared to students of the same grade nationally. The National Percentile range indicates that if this student had taken the test numerous times the scores would have fallen within the range shown. The shaded area on the graph represents the average range of scores, usually defined as the middle 50 percent of students nationally. Scores in the area to the right of the shading are above the average range. Scores in the area to the left of the shading are below the average range.

In Reading, for example, this student achieved a National Percentile rank of 65. This student scored higher than 65 percent of the students nationally. This score is in the average range. This student has a total of five scores in the average range. One score is in the above average range. No scores are in the below average range.

Performance on Objectives

The next section of the report presents performance on the objectives. Each objective is measured by a minimum of 4 items. The Objectives Performance Index (OPI) provides an estimate of the number of items that a student could be expected to answer correctly if there had been 100 items for that objective. The OPI is used to indicate mastery of each objective. An OPI of 75 and above characterizes Mastery. An OPI between 50 and 74 indicates Partial Mastery, and an OPI below 50 indicates Non-Mastery. The two-digit number preceding the objective title identifies the objective, which is fully described in the Teacher's Guide to *TerraNova*. The bands on either side of the diamonds indicate the range within which the student's test scores would fall if the student were tested numerous times.

In Reading, for example, this student could be expected to respond correctly to 91 out of 100 items measuring Basic Understanding. If this student had taken the test numerous times the OPI for this objective would have fallen between 82 and 93.

Teacher Notes

MULTIPLE ASSESSMENTS

Individual Profile Report

MARY BROWN

Grade 7

Purpose

The Observations section of the Individual Profile Report gives teachers and parents information to interpret this report. This page is a narrative description of the data on the other side.

Simulated Data

Birthdate: 09/11/82
Special Codes:
A B C D E F G H I J K L M N O P Q R S T
4 0 2 2 6   1 2 1
Form/Level: A-17

Test Date: 11/01/99   Scoring: PATTERN (IRT)
QM: 08   Norms Date: 1996

Class: PARKER
School: WINFIELD
District: WINFIELD

City/State: WINFIELD, CA

CTB
McGraw-Hill

Page 2

Figure 4 (Source: CTB/McGraw-Hill, copyright © 1997. All rights reserved. Reproduced with permission.)

TerraNova

MULTIPLE ASSESSMENTS

Student Performance Level Report

KEN ALLEN

Grade 4

Purpose

This report describes this student's achievement in terms of five performance levels for each content area. The meaning of these levels is described on the back of this page. Performance levels are a new way of describing achievement.

Simulated Data

Birthdate: 02/08/86
Special Codes:
A B C D E F G H I J K L M N O P Q R S T
3 5 9 7 3 2   1 1 1
Form/Level: A-14
Test Date: 04/15/97   Scoring PATTERN (IRT)
QM: 31   Norms Date: 1996

Class: SCHWARZ
School: WINFIELD
District: GREEN VALLEY

City/State: WINFIELD, CA

CTB McGraw-Hill   *Page 1*   Copyright © 1997 CTB/McGraw-Hill. All rights reserved.

Performance Levels	Reading	Language	Mathematics	Science	Social Studies
5 Advanced					
4 Proficient					
3 Nearing Proficiency	✓				✓
2 Progressing	✓	✓	✓	✓	✓
1 Step 1	✓	✓	✓	✓	✓

(Partially Proficient)

Observations

Performance level scores provide a measure of what students *can do* in terms of the content and skills assessed by *TerraNova*, and typically found in curricula for Grades 3, 4, and 5. It is desirable to work towards achieving a Level 4 (Proficient) or Level 5 (Advanced) by the end of Grade 5.

The number of check marks indicates the performance level this student reached in each content area. For example, this student reached Level 3 in Reading and Social Studies.

The performance level indicates this student can perform the majority of what is described for that level and even more of what is described for the levels below. The student may also be capable of performing some of the things described in the next higher level, but not enough to have reached that level of performance.

For example, this student can perform the majority of what is described for Level 3 in Reading and even more of what is described for Level 2 and Level 1 in Reading. This student may also be capable of performing some of what is described for Level 4 in Reading.

For each content area look at the skills and knowledge described in the next higher level. These are the competencies this student needs to demonstrate to show academic growth.

Figure 5   (SOURCE: CTB/McGraw-Hill, copyright © 1997. All rights reserved. Reproduced with permission.)

Performance Levels (Grades 3, 4, 5)	Reading	Language	Mathematics	Science	Social Studies
5 Advanced	Students use analogies to generalize. They identify a paraphrase of concepts or ideas in texts. They can indicate thought processes that led them to a previous answer. In written responses, they demonstrate understanding of an implied theme, assess intent of passage information, and provide justification as well as support for their answers.	Students understand logical development in paragraph structure. They identify essential information from notes. They recognize the effect of prepositional phrases on subject-verb agreement. They find and correct at least 4 out of 6 errors when editing simple narratives. They correct run-on and incomplete sentences in more complex texts. They can eliminate all errors when editing their own work.	Students locate decimals on a number line; compute with decimals and fractions; read scale drawings; find areas; identify geometric transformations; construct and label bar graphs; find simple probabilities; find averages; use patterns in data to solve problems; use multiple strategies and concepts to solve unfamiliar problems; express mathematical ideas and explain the problem-solving process.	Students understand a broad range of grade level scientific concepts, such as the structure of Earth and instinctive behavior. They know terminology, such as decomposers, fossil fuel, eclipse, and buoyancy. Knowledge of more complex environmental issues includes, for example, the positive consequences of a forest fire. Students can process and interpret more detailed tables and graphs. They can suggest improvements to experimental design, such as running more trials.	Students consistently demonstrate skills such as synthesizing information from two sources (e.g., a document and a map). They show understanding of the democratic process and global environmental issues, and know the location of continents and major countries. They analyze and summarize information from multiple sources in early American history. They thoroughly explain both sides of an issue and give complete and detailed written answers to questions.
4 Proficient	Students interpret figures of speech. They recognize paraphrase of text information and retrieve information to complete forms. In more complex texts, they identify themes, main ideas, or author purpose/point of view. They analyze and apply information in graphic and text form, and draw reasonable generalizations, and draw conclusions. In written responses, they can identify key elements from text.	Students select the best supporting sentences for a topic sentence. They use compound predicates to combine sentences. They identify simple subjects and predicates, recognize correct usage when confronted with two types of errors, and find and correct at least 3 out of 6 errors when editing simple narratives. They can edit their own work with only minor errors.	Students compare, order, and round whole numbers; know place value to thousands; identify fractions; use computation and estimation strategies; relate multiplication to addition; measure to nearest half-inch and centimeter; measure and find perimeters; estimate measures; find elapsed times; combine and subdivide shapes; identify parallel lines; interpret tables and graphs; solve two-step problems.	Students have a range of specific science knowledge, including details about animal adaptations and classification, states of matter, and the geology of Earth. They recognize scientific words such as habitat, gravity, and mass. They understand the usefulness of computers. They understand reasons for conserving natural resources. Understanding of experimentation includes analyzing purpose, interpreting data, and selecting tools to gather data.	Students demonstrate skills such as making inferences, using historical documents and analyzing maps to determine the economic strengths of a region. They understand the function of currency in various cultures and supply and demand. They summarize information from multiple sources, recognize relationships, determine relevance of information, and show global awareness. They propose solutions to real-world problems and support ideas with appropriate details.
3 Nearing Proficiency	Students use context clues and structural analysis to determine word meaning. They recognize homonyms and antonyms in grade-level text. They identify important details, sequence, cause and effect, and lessons embedded in the text. They interpret characters' feelings and apply information to new situations. In written responses, they can express an opinion and support it.	Students identify irrelevant sentences in paragraphs and select the best place to insert new information. They recognize faulty sentence construction. They can combine simple sentences with conjunctions and use simple subordination of phrases/clauses. They identify reference sources. They recognize correct conventions for dates, closings, and place names in informal correspondence.	Students identify even and odd numbers; subtract whole numbers with regrouping; multiply and divide by one-digit numbers; identify simple fractions; measure with ruler to nearest inch; tell time to nearest fifteen minutes; recognize and classify common shapes; recognize symmetry; subdivide shapes; complete bar graphs; extend numerical and geometric patterns; apply simple logical reasoning.	Students are familiar with the life cycles of plants and animals. They can identify an example of a cold-blooded animal. They infer what once existed from fossil evidence. They recognize the term habitat. They understand the water cycle. They know science and society issues such as recycling and sources of pollution. They extrapolate data, devise a simple classification scheme, and determine the purpose of a simple experiment.	Students demonstrate skills in organizing information. They use time lines, product and global maps, and cardinal directions. They understand simple cause and effect relationships and historical documents. They sequence events, associate holidays with events, and classify natural resources. They compare life in different times and understand some economic concepts related to products, jobs, and the environment. They give some detail in written responses.
2 Progressing	Students identify synonyms for grade-level words, and use context clues to define common words. They make simple inferences and predictions based on text. They identify characters' feelings. They can transfer information from text to graphic form, or from graphic form to text. In written responses, they can provide limited support for their answers.	Students identify the use of correct verb tenses and supply verbs to complete sentences. They complete paragraphs by selecting an appropriate topic sentence. They select correct adjective forms.	Students know ordinal numbers; solve coin combination problems; count by tens; add whole numbers with regrouping; have basic estimation skills; understand addition property of zero; write and identify number sentences describing simple situations; read calendars; identify appropriate measurement tools; recognize congruent figures; use simple coordinate grids; read common tables and graphs.	Students recognize that plants decompose and become part of soil. They can classify a plant as a vegetable. They recognize that camouflage relates to survival. They recognize science terms such as hibernate. They have an understanding of human impact on the environment and are familiar with causes of pollution. They find the correct bar graph to represent given data and transfer data appropriate for middle elementary grades to a bar graph.	Students demonstrate simple information-processing skills such as using basic maps and keys. They recognize simple geographical terms, types of jobs, modes of transportation, and natural resources. They connect a human need with an appropriate community service. They identify some early famous presidents and know the capital of the United States. Their written answers are partially complete.
1 Step 1	Students select pictured representations of ideas and identify stated details contained in simple texts. In written responses, they can select and transfer information from charts.	Students supply subjects to complete sentences. They identify the correct use of pronouns. They edit for the correct use of end marks and initial capital letters, and identify the correct convention for greetings in letters.	Students read and recognize numbers to 1000; identify real-world use of numbers; add and subtract two-digit numbers without regrouping; identify addition situations; recognize and complete simple geometric and numerical patterns.	Students recognize basic adaptations for living in the water, identify an animal that is hatched from an egg, and associate an organism with its correct environment. They identify an object as metal. They have some understanding of conditions on the moon. They supply one way a computer can be useful. They associate an instrument like a telescope with a field of study.	Students are developing fundamental social studies skills such as locating and classifying basic information. They locate information in pictures and read and complete simple bar graphs related to social studies concepts and contexts. They can connect some city buildings with their functions and recognize certain historical objects.

Partially Proficient (bracket covering levels 3, 2, 1)

W1 SPLR P2:11/02

IMPORTANT: Each performance level, depicted on the other side, indicates the student can perform the majority of what is described for that level and even more of what is described for the levels below. The student may also be capable of performing some of the things described in the next higher level, but not enough to have reached that level.

Figure 6 (Source: CTB/McGraw-Hill, copyright © 1997. All rights reserved. Reproduced with permission.)

confidence interval. In these reports, we usually report either a 90 percent or 95 percent confidence interval. Interpret a confidence interval this way: Suppose we report a 90 percent confidence interval of 25 to 37. This means we estimate that, if the child took the test multiple times, we would expect that child's score to be in the 25 to 37 range 90 percent of the time.

Now look under the section titled Norm-Referenced Scores on the first page of the Individual Profile Report (Figure 3). The farthest column on the right provides the NP Range, which is the National Percentile scores represented by the score bands in the chart.

Next notice the column labeled Grade Equivalent. Theoretically, grade level equivalents equate a student's score in a skill area with the average grade placement of children who made the same score. Many psychologists and test developers would prefer that we stopped reporting grade equivalents, because they can be grossly misleading. For example, the average reading grade level of high school seniors as reported by one of the more popular tests is the eighth grade level. Does that mean that the nation's high school seniors cannot read? No. The way the test publisher calculated grade equivalents was to determine the average test scores for students in grades 4 to 6 and then simply extend the resulting prediction formula to grades 7 to 12. The result is that parents of average high school seniors who take the test in question would mistakenly believe that their seniors are reading four grade levels behind! Stick to the percentile in interpreting your child's scores.

Now look at the columns labeled Scale Score and National Stanine. These are two of a group of scores we also call *standard scores.* In reports for other tests, you may see other standard scores reported, such as Normal Curve Equivalents (NCEs), Z-Scores, and T-Scores. The IQ that we report on intelligence tests, for example, is a standard score. Standard scores are simply a way of expressing a student's scores in terms of the statistical properties of the scores from the norm group against which we are comparing the child. Although most psychologists prefer to speak in terms of standard scores among themselves, parents are advised to stick to percentiles in interpreting your child's performance.

Now look at the section of the report labeled Performance on Objectives. In this section, the test publisher reports how your child did on the various skills that make up each skills area. Note that the scores on each objective are expressed as a percentile band, and you are again told whether your child's score constitutes mastery, non-mastery, or partial mastery. Note that these scores are made up of tallies of sometimes small numbers of test items taken from sections such as Reading or Math. Because they are calculated from a much smaller number of scores than the main scales are (for example, Sentence Comprehension is made up of fewer items than overall Reading), their scores are less reliable than those of the main scales.

Now look at the second page of the Individual Profile Report (Figure 4). Here the test publisher provides a narrative summary of how the child did on the test. These summaries are computer-generated according to rules provided by the publisher. Note that the results descriptions are more general than those on the previous three report pages. But they allow the teacher to form a general picture of which students are performing at what general skill levels.

Finally, your child's guidance counselor may receive a summary report such as the TerraNova Student Performance Level Report. (See Figures 5 and 6.) In this report, the publisher explains to school personnel what skills the test assessed and generally how proficiently the child tested under each skill.

Which States Require Which Tests

Tables 1 through 3 summarize standardized testing practices in the 50 states and the District of Columbia. This information is constantly changing; the information presented here was accurate as of the date of printing of this book. Many states have changed their testing practices in response to revised accountability legislation, while others have changed the tests they use.

Table 1   State Web Sites: Education and Testing

STATE	GENERAL WEB SITE	STATE TESTING WEB SITE
Alabama	http://www.alsde.edu/	http://www.fairtest.org/states/al.htm
Alaska	www.educ.state.ak.us/	http://www.eed.state.ak.us/tls/Performance Standards/
Arizona	http://www.ade.state.az.us/	http://www.ade.state.az.us/standards/
Arkansas	http://arkedu.k12.ar.us/	http://www.fairtest.org/states/ar.htm
California	http://goldmine.cde.ca.gov/	http://ww.cde.ca.gov/cilbranch/sca/
Colorado	http://www.cde.state.co.us/index_home.htm	http://www.cde.state.co.us/index_assess.htm
Connecticut	http://www.state.ct.us/sde	http://www.state.ct.us/sde/cmt/index.htm
Delaware	http://www.doe.state.de.us/	http://www.doe.state.de.us/aab/index.htm
District of Columbia	http://www.k12.dc.us/dcps/home.html	http://www.k12.dc.us/dcps/data/data_frame2.html
Florida	http://www.firn.edu/doe/	http://www.firn.edu/doe/sas/sasshome.htm
Georgia	http://www.doe.k12.ga.us/	http://www.doe.k12.ga.us/sla/ret/recotest.html
Hawaii	http://kalama.doe.hawaii.edu/upena/	http://www.fairtest.org/states/hi.htm
Idaho	http://www.sde.state.id.us/Dept/	http://www.sde.state.id.us/instruct/ schoolaccount/statetesting.htm
Illinois	http://www.isbe.state.il.us/	http://www.isbe.state.il.us/isat/
Indiana	http://doe.state.in.us/	http://doe.state.in.us/assessment/welcome.html
Iowa	http://www.state.ia.us/educate/index.html	(Tests Chosen Locally)
Kansas	http://www.ksbe.state.ks.us/	http://www.ksbe.state.ks.us/assessment/
Kentucky	htp://www.kde.state.ky.us/	http://www.kde.state.ky.us/oaa/
Louisiana	http://www.doe.state.la.us/DOE/asps/home.asp	http://www.doe.state.la.us/DOE/asps/home.asp? I=HISTAKES
Maine	http://janus.state.me.us/education/homepage.htm	http://janus.state.me.us/education/mea/ meacompass.htm
Maryland	http://www.msde.state.md.us/	http://www.fairtest.org/states/md.htm
Massachusetts	http://www.doe.mass.edu/	http://www.doe.mass.edu/mcas/
Michigan	http://www.mde.state.mi.us/	http://www.mde.state.mi.us/off/meap/

STATE	GENERAL WEB SITE	STATE TESTING WEB SITE
Minnesota	http://www.educ.state.mn.us/	http://fairtest.org/states/mn.htm
Mississippi	http://mdek12.state.ms.us/	http://fairtest.org/states/ms.htm
Missouri	http://services.dese.state.mo.us/	http://fairtest.org/states/mo.htm
Montana	http://www.metnet.mt.gov/	http://fairtest.org/states/mt.htm
Nebraska	http://nde4.nde.state.ne.us/	http://www.edneb.org/IPS/AppAccrd/ApprAccrd.html
Nevada	http://www.nsn.k12.nv.us/nvdoe/	http://www.nsn.k12.nv.us/nvdoe/reports/TerraNova.doc
New Hampshire	http://www.state.nh.us/doe/	http://www.state.nh.us/doe/Assessment/assessme(NHEIAP).htm
New Jersey	http://ww.state.nj.us/education/	http://www.state.nj.us/njded/stass/index.html
New Mexico	http://sde.state.nm.us/	http://sde.state.nm.us/press/august30a.html
New York	http://www.nysed.gov/	http://www.emsc.nysed.gov/ciai/assess.html
North Carolina	http://www.dpi.state.nc.us/	http://www.dpi.state.nc.us/accountability/reporting/index.html
North Dakota	http://www.dpi.state.nd.us/dpi/index.htm	http://www.dpi.state.nd.us/dpi/reports/assess/assess.htm
Ohio	http://www.ode.state.oh.us/	http://www.ode.state.oh.us/ca/
Oklahoma	http://sde.state.ok.us/	http://sde.state.ok.us/acrob/testpack.pdf
Oregon	http://www.ode.state.or.us//	http://www.ode.state.or.us/assmt/index.htm
Pennsylvania	http://www.pde.psu.edu/ http://instruct.ride.ri.net/ride_home_page.html	http://www.fairtest.org/states/pa.htm
Rhode Island		
South Carolina	http://www.state.sc.us/sde/	http://www.state.sc.us/sde/reports/terranov.htm
South Dakota	http://www.state.sd.us/state/executive/deca/	http://www.state.sd.us/state/executive/deca/TA/McRelReport/McRelReports.htm
Tennessee	http://www.state.tn.us/education/	http://www.state.tn.us/education/tsintro.htm
Texas	http://www.tea.state.tx.us/	http://www.tea.state.tx.us/student.assessment/
Utah	http://www.usoe.k12.ut.us/	http://www.usoe.k12.ut.us/eval.usoeeval.htm
Vermont	http://www.cit.state.vt.us/educ/	http://www.fairtest.org/states/vt.htm

STATE	GENERAL WEB SITE	STATE TESTING WEB SITE
Virginia	http://www.pen.k12.va.us/Anthology/VDOE/	http://www.pen.k12.va.us/VDOE/Assessment/home.shtml
Washington	http://www.k12.wa.us/	http://assessment.ospi.wednet.edu/
West Virginia	http://wvde.state.wv.us/	http://www.fairtest.org/states/wv.htm
Wisconsin	http://www.dpi.state.wi.us/	http://www.dpi.state.wi.us/dpi/oea/spr_kce.html
Wyoming	http://www.k12.wy.us/wdehome.html	http://www.asme.com/wycas/index.htm

Table 2 Norm-Referenced and Criterion-Referenced Tests Administered by State

STATE	NORM-REFERENCED TEST	CRITERION-REFERENCED TEST	EXIT EXAM
Alabama	Stanford Achievement Test		Alabama High School Graduation Exam
Alaska	California Achievement Test		
Arizona	Stanford Achievement Test	Arizona's Instrument to Measure Standards (AIMS)	
Arkansas	Stanford Achievement Test		
California	Stanford Achievement Test	Standardized Testing and Reporting Supplement	High School Exit Exam (HSEE)
Colorado	None	Colorado Student Assessment Program	
Connecticut		Connecticut Mastery Test	
Delaware	Stanford Achievement Test	Delaware Student Testing Program	
District of Columbia	Stanford Achievement Test		
Florida	(Locally Selected)	Florida Comprehensive Assessment Test (FCAT)	High School Competency Test (HSCT)
Georgia	Iowa Tests of Basic Skills	Criterion-Referenced Competency Tests (CRCT)	Georgia High School Graduation Tests
Hawaii	Stanford Achievement Test	Credit by Examination	Hawaii State Test of Essential Competencies
Idaho	Iowa Test of Basic Skills/ Tests of Direct Achievement and Proficiency	Writing/Mathematics Assessment	
Illinois		Illinois Standards Achievement Tests	Prairie State Achievement Examination
Indiana		Indiana Statewide Testing for Education Progress	
Iowa	(None)		
Kansas		(State-Developed Tests)	
Kentucky	Comprehensive Tests of Basic Skills	Kentucky Instructional Results Information System	
Louisiana	Iowa Tests of Basic Skills	Louisiana Educational Assessment Program	Graduate Exit Exam
Maine		Maine Educational Assessment	
Maryland		Maryland School Performance Assessment Program	
Massachusetts		Massachusetts Comprehensive Assessment System	

STATE	NORM-REFERENCED TEST	CRITERION-REFERENCED TEST	EXIT EXAM
Michigan		Michigan Educational Assessment Program	High School Test
Minnesota		Basic Standards Test	Profile of Learning
Mississippi	Iowa Test of Basic Skills	Subject Area Testing Program	Functional Literacy Examination
Missouri		Missouri Mastery and Achievement Test	
Montana	(districts' choice)		
Nebraska			
Nevada	TerraNova		Nevada High School Proficiency Examination
New Hampshire		NH Educational Improvement and Assessment Program	
New Jersey		Elementary School Proficiency Test/Early Warning Test	High School Proficiency Test
New Mexico	TerraNova		New Mexico High School Competency Exam
New York		Pupil Evaluation Program/ Preliminary Competency Test	Regents Competency Tests
North Carolina	Iowa Test of Basic Skills	NC End of Grade Test	
North Dakota	TerraNova	ND Reading, Writing Speaking, Listening, Math Test	
Ohio		Ohio Proficiency Tests	Ohio Proficiency Tests
Oklahoma	Iowa Tests of Basic Skills	Oklahoma Criterion-Referenced Tests	
Oregon		Oregon Statewide Assessment	
Pennsylvania		Pennsylvania System of School Assessment	
Rhode Island	Metropolitan Achievement Test		
South Carolina	TerraNova	Palmetto Achievement Challenge Tests	High School Exit Exam
South Dakota	Stanford Achievement Test		
Tennessee	Tennessee Comprehensive Assessment Program	Tennessee Comprehensive Assessment Program	
Texas		Texas Assessment of Academic Skills	Texas Assessment of Academic Skills
Utah	Stanford Achievement Test	Core Curriculum Testing	

STATE	NORM-REFERENCED TEST	CRITERION-REFERENCED TEST	EXIT EXAM
Vermont		New Standards Reference Exams	
Virginia	Stanford Achievement Test	Virginia Standards of Learning	Virginia Standards of Learning
Washington	Iowa Tests of Basic Skills	Washington Assessment of Student Learning	Washington Assessment of Student Learning
West Virginia	Stanford Achievement Test		
Wisconsin	TerraNova	Wisconsin Knowledge and Concepts Examinations	
Wyoming	TerraNova	Wyoming Comprehensive Assessment System	Wyoming Comprehensive Assessment System

Table 3 Standardized Test Schedules by State

STATE	KG	1	2	3	4	5	6	7	8	9	10	11	12	COMMENT
Alabama				X	X	X	X	X	X	X	X	X	X	
Alaska				X					X		X			
Arizona			X	X	X	X	X	X	X	X	X	X	X	
Arkansas				X	X			X	X		X	X	X	
California			X	X	X	X	X	X	X	X	X	X		
Colorado				X	X			X						
Connecticut					X		X		X					
Delaware				X	X	X			X		X	X		
District of Columbia		X	X	X	X	X	X	X	X	X	X			
Florida		X	X	X	X	X	X	X	X	X	X	X	X	There is no state-mandated norm-referenced testing. However, the state collects information furnished by local districts that elect to perform norm-referenced testing. The FCAT is administered to Grades 4, 8, and 10 to assess reading and Grades 5, 8, and 10 to assess math.
Georgia				X			X		X					
Hawaii				X			X		X		X			The Credit by Examination is voluntary and is given in Grade 8 in Algebra and Foreign Languages.
Idaho				X	X	X	X	X	X	X	X	X		
Illinois				X	X		X	X	X		X	X		Exit Exam failure will not disqualify students from graduation if all other requirements are met.
Indiana				X			X		X		X			
Iowa		*	*	*	*	*	*	*	*	*	*	*	*	*Iowa does not currently have a statewide testing program. Locally chosen assessments are administered to grades determined locally.
Kansas				X	X	X		X	X		X			

STATE	KG	1	2	3	4	5	6	7	8	9	10	11	12	COMMENT
Kentucky					X	X		X	X			X	X	
Louisiana				X		X	X	X		X				
Maine					X				X			X		
Maryland				X		X			X					
Massachusetts					X				X		X			
Michigan					X	X		X	X					
Minnesota				X		X			X					Testing Information from Fair Test.Org. There was no readily accessible state-sponsored site.
Mississippi					X	X	X	X	X					State's Web site refused connection; all data were obtained from FairTest.Org.
Missouri			X	X	X	X	X	X	X	X	X			
Montana					X				X			X		The State Board of Education has decided to use a single norm-referenced test statewide beginning 2000–2001 school year.
Nebraska		**	**	**	**	**	**	**	**	**	**	**	**	**Decisions regarding testing are left to the individual school districts.
Nevada					X				X					Districts choose whether and how to test with norm-referenced tests.
New Hampshire				X			X				X			
New Jersey				X	X			X	X	X	X	X		
New Mexico					X		X		X					
New York					X				X	X				Assessment program is going through major revisions.
North Carolina				X	X	X	X	X	X		X			NRT Testing selects samples of students, not all.
North Dakota					X		X		X		X			
Ohio					X		X			X			X	
Oklahoma				X		X		X	X			X		
Oregon				X		X			X		X			

STATE	KG	1	2	3	4	5	6	7	8	9	10	11	12	COMMENT
Pennsylvania						X	X		X	X		X		
Rhode Island				X	X	X		X	X	X	X			
South Carolina				X	X	X	X	X	X	X	X			
South Dakota			X		X	X			X	X		X		
Tennessee			X	X	X	X	X	X	X			X		
Texas				X	X	X	X	X	X		X			
Utah		X	X	X	X	X	X	X	X	X	X	X	X	
Vermont					X	X	X		X	X	X	X		Rated by FairTest.Org as a nearly model system for assessment.
Virginia				X	X	X	X		X	X		X		
Washington					X			X			X			
West Virginia		X	X	X	X	X	X	X	X	X	X	X		
Wisconsin					X				X		X			
Wyoming					X				X			X		

Testing Accommodations

The more testing procedures vary from one classroom or school to the next, the less we can compare the scores from one group to another. Consider a test in which the publisher recommends that three sections of the test be given in one 45-minute session per day on three consecutive days. School A follows those directions. To save time, School B gives all three sections of the test in one session lasting slightly more than two hours. We can't say that both schools followed the same testing procedures. Remember that the test publishers provide testing procedures so schools can administer the tests in as close a manner as possible to the way the tests were administered to the groups used to obtain test norms. When we compare students' scores to norms, we want to compare apples to apples, not apples to oranges.

Most schools justifiably resist making any changes in testing procedures. Informally, a teacher can make minor changes that don't alter the testing procedures, such as separating two students who talk with each other instead of paying attention to the test; letting Lisa, who is getting over an ear infection, sit closer to the front so she can hear better; or moving Jeffrey away from the window to prevent his looking out the window and daydreaming.

There are two groups of students who require more formal testing accommodations. One group of students is identified as having a disability under Section 504 of the Rehabilitation Act of 1973 (Public Law 93-112). These students face

some challenge but, with reasonable and appropriate accommodation, can take advantage of the same educational opportunities as other students. That is, they have a condition that requires some accommodation for them.

Just as schools must remove physical barriers to accommodate students with disabilities, they must make appropriate accommodations to remove other types of barriers to students' access to education. Marie is profoundly deaf, even with strong hearing aids. She does well in school with the aid of an interpreter, who signs her teacher's instructions to her and tells her teacher what Marie says in reply. An appropriate accommodation for Marie would be to provide the interpreter to sign test instructions to her, or to allow her to watch a videotape with an interpreter signing test instructions. Such a reasonable accommodation would not deviate from standard testing procedures and, in fact, would ensure that Marie received the same instructions as the other students.

If your child is considered disabled and has what is generally called a Section 504 Plan or individual accommodation plan (IAP), then the appropriate way to ask for testing accommodations is to ask for them in a meeting to discuss school accommodations under the plan. If your child is not already covered by such a plan, he or she won't qualify for one merely because you request testing accommodations.

The other group of students who may receive formal testing accommodations are those identified as handicapped under the Individuals with Disabilities Education Act (IDEA)—students with mental retardation, learning disabilities, serious emotional disturbance, orthopedic handicap, hearing or visual problems, and other handicaps defined in the law. These students have been identified under procedures governed by federal and sometimes state law, and their education is governed by a document called the Individualized Educational Program (IEP). Unless you are under a court order specifically revoking your educational rights on behalf of your child, you are a full member of the IEP team even if you and your child's other parent are divorced and the other parent has custody. Until recently, IEP teams actually had the prerogative to exclude certain handicapped students from taking standardized group testing altogether. However, today states make it more difficult to exclude students from testing.

If your child is classified as handicapped and has an IEP, the appropriate place to ask for testing accommodations is in an IEP team meeting. In fact, federal regulations require IEP teams to address testing accommodations. You have the right to call a meeting at any time. In that meeting, you will have the opportunity to present your case for the accommodations you believe are necessary. Be prepared for the other team members to resist making extreme accommodations unless you can present a very strong case. If your child is identified as handicapped and you believe that he or she should be provided special testing accommodations, contact the person at your child's school who is responsible for convening IEP meetings and request a meeting to discuss testing accommodations.

Problems arise when a request is made for accommodations that cause major departures from standard testing procedures. For example, Lynn has an identified learning disability in mathematics calculation and attends resource classes for math. Her disability is so severe that her IEP calls for her to use a calculator when performing all math problems. She fully under-stands math concepts, but she simply can't perform the calculations without the aid of a calculator. Now it's time for Lynn to take the school-based standardized tests, and she asks to use a calculator. In this case, since her IEP already requires her to be provided with a calculator when performing math calculations, she may be allowed a calculator during school standardized tests. However, because using a calculator constitutes a major violation of standard testing procedures, her score on all sections in which she is allowed to use a calculator will be recorded as a failure, and her results in some states will be removed from among those of other students in her school in calculating school results.

How do we determine whether a student is allowed formal accommodations in standardized school testing and what these accommodations may be? First, if your child is not already identified as either handicapped or disabled, having the child classified in either group solely to receive testing accommodations will be considered a violation of the laws governing both classifications. Second, even if your child is already classified in either group, your state's department of public instruction will provide strict guidelines for the testing accommodations schools may make. Third, even if your child is classified in either group and you are proposing testing accommodations allowed under state testing guidelines, any accommodations must still be both *reasonable* and *appropriate*. To be reasonable and appropriate, testing accommodations must relate to your child's disability and must be similar to those already in place in his or her daily educational program. If your child is always tested individually in a separate room for all tests in all subjects, then a similar practice in taking school-based standardized tests may be appropriate. But if your child has a learning disability only in mathematics calculation, requesting that all test questions be read to him or her is inappropriate because that accommodation does not relate to his identified handicap.

Glossary

Accountability The idea that a school district is held responsible for the achievement of its students. The term may also be applied to holding students responsible for a certain level of achievement in order to be promoted or to graduate.

Achievement test An assessment that measures current knowledge in one or more of the areas taught in most schools, such as reading, math, and language arts.

Aptitude test An assessment designed to predict a student's potential for learning knowledge or skills.

Content validity The extent to which a test represents the content it is designed to cover.

Criterion-referenced test A test that rates how thoroughly a student has mastered a specific skill or area of knowledge. Typically, a criterion-referenced test is subjective, and relies on someone to observe and rate student work; it doesn't allow for easy comparisons of achievement among students. Performance assessments are criterion-referenced tests. The opposite of a criterion-referenced test is a norm-referenced test.

Frequency distribution A tabulation of individual scores (or groups of scores) that shows the number of persons who obtained each score.

Generalizability The idea that the score on a test reflects what a child knows about a subject, or how well he performs the skills the test is supposed to be assessing. Generalizability requires that enough test items are administered to truly assess a student's achievement.

Grade equivalent A score on a scale developed to indicate the school grade (usually measured in months of a year) that corresponds to an average chronological age, mental age, test score, or other characteristic. A grade equivalent of 6.4 is interpreted as a score that is average for a group in the fourth month of Grade 6.

High-stakes assessment A type of standardized test that has major consequences for a student or school (such as whether a child graduates from high school or gets admitted to college).

Mean Average score of a group of scores.

Median The middle score in a set of scores ranked from smallest to largest.

National percentile Percentile score derived from the performance of a group of individuals across the nation.

Normative sample A comparison group consisting of individuals who have taken a test under standard conditions.

Norm-referenced test A standardized test that can compare scores of students in one school with a reference group (usually other students in the same grade and age, called the "norm group"). Norm-referenced tests compare the achievement of one student or the students of a school, school district, or state with the norm score.

Norms A summary of the performance of a group of individuals on which a test was standardized.

Percentile An incorrect form of the word *centile,* which is the percent of a group of scores that falls below a given score. Although the correct term is *centile,* much of the testing literature has adopted the term *percentile.*

Performance standards A level of performance on a test set by education experts.

Quartiles Points that divide the frequency distribution of scores into equal fourths.

Regression to the mean The tendency of scores in a group of scores to vary in the direction of the mean. For example: If a child has an abnormally low score on a test, she is likely to make a higher score (that is, one closer to the mean) the next time she takes the test.

Reliability The consistency with which a test measures some trait or characteristic. A measure can be reliable without being valid, but it can't be valid without being reliable.

Standard deviation A statistical measure used to describe the extent to which scores vary in a group of scores. Approximately 68 percent of scores in a group are expected to be in a range from one standard deviation below the mean to one standard deviation above the mean.

Standardized test A test that contains well-defined questions of proven validity and that produces reliable scores. Such tests are commonly paper-and-pencil exams containing multiple-choice items, true or false questions, matching exercises, or short fill-in-the-blanks items. These tests may also include performance assessment items (such as a writing sample), but assessment items cannot be completed quickly or scored reliably.

Test anxiety Anxiety that occurs in test-taking situations. Test anxiety can seriously impair individuals' ability to obtain accurate scores on a test.

Validity The extent to which a test measures the trait or characteristic it is designed to measure. Also see *reliability.*

Answer Keys for Practice Skills

Chapter 2: Vocabulary

1	A
2	B
3	D
4	B
5	B
6	C
7	A
8	B
9	B
10	D
11	B
12	D
13	C
14	A
15	C
16	B
17	C
18	B
19	C
20	A

Chapter 3: Reading Comprehension

1	B
2	B
3	C
4	A
5	C
6	C
7	B
8	B
9	B
10	A
11	B
12	C
13	D
14	A

Chapter 4: Language Mechanics

1	C
2	C
3	D
4	B
5	C
6	C
7	A
8	A
9	C
10	C
11	C

Chapter 5: Language Expression

1	D
2	C
3	A
4	A
5	C
6	C
7	B
8	B
9	D
10	C
11	B
12	B
13	B
14	B
15	D
16	D
17	B
18	D

Chapter 6: Spelling and Study Skills

1	B
2	C
3	C
4	E
5	A
6	C
7	D
8	C
9	C
10	C
11	D
12	C
13	D
14	C
15	B
16	D
17	B
18	C
19	C
20	C

Chapter 7: Math Concepts

1	B
2	C
3	A
4	D
5	B
6	C
7	D
8	A
9	C
10	C
11	C
12	D
13	C
14	B
15	D
16	C
17	B
18	D
19	B
20	A
21	C
22	B
23	C
24	B
25	B
26	B

27	C	9	B	3	A	16	D
28	A	10	C	4	C	17	D
		11	C	5	B	18	A
		12	A	6	C	19	C
		13	E	7	B	20	B

Chapter 8:
Math Computation

		14	C	8	B	21	D
1	A	15	D	9	B	22	B
2	B	16	A	10	C	23	A
3	A			11	D	24	C
4	D			12	B	25	D
5	B			13	D	26	E

Chapter 9:
Math Applications

6	C		
7	A	1	B
8	E	2	B
		14	A
		15	D

Sample Practice Test

The test questions given here are designed to provide a sample of the kinds of items fourth-grade students may encounter on a standardized test. They are *not* identical to any standardized test your child will take. However, the questions cover all the areas discussed in this book and provide a review that is similar in format to a standardized test.

The sample test provides 103 questions organized by skill areas presented in the preceding chapters. It is intended to provide a rough idea about the types of test questions your child will probably encounter on the commercial standardized tests provided at school. It is not an exact copy.

How to Use the Test

In this guide, we have been more concerned with strengthening certain skills than with the ability to work under time constraints. We don't recommend that you attempt to simulate actual testing conditions. Here are four alternative ways of using this test:

1. Administer this test to your child after you have completed all skills chapters and have begun to implement the strategies we suggested. Allow your child to work at a leisurely pace, probably consisting of 20- to 30-minute sessions spread out over several days.

2. Administer the pertinent section of the test after you have gone through each chapter and implemented the strategies.

3. Use the test as a pretest rather than as a posttest, administering the entire test in 20- to 30-minute sessions spread out over several days to identify the skills on which your child needs the most work. Then concentrate most of your efforts on the skills on which your child scores the lowest.

4. Administer each section of the test before you go through each chapter as a kind of skills check to help you determine how much of your energy you need to devote to that skill area.

Administering the Test

Don't provide any help to your child during the test, but note specific problems. For example, if your child has problems reading math sentences, note whether the problem is with reading rather than with math. If your child's answers look sloppy, with many erasures or cross-outs, note that you need to work on neatness. (Remember that tests administered at school will be machine-scored, and the scanners sometimes mistake sloppily erased answers as the answers the child intends.)

To the Student:

These tests will give you a chance to put the tips you have learned to work.
A few last reminders . . .

- Be sure you understand all the directions before you begin each test. You may ask the teacher questions about the directions if you do not understand them.

- Work as quickly as you can during each test.

- When you change an answer, be sure to erase your first mark completely.

- You can guess at an answer or skip difficult items and go back to them later.

- Use the tips you have learned whenever you can.

- It is OK to be a little nervous. You may even do better.

Now that you have completed the lessons in this book, you are on your way to scoring high!

STUDENT'S NAME

LAST   FIRST   MI

SCHOOL

TEACHER

FEMALE ◯   MALE ◯

BIRTHDATE

MONTH	DAY	YEAR

JAN ◯	⓪ ⓪	⓪
FEB ◯	① ①	①
MAR ◯	② ②	②
APR ◯	③ ③	③
MAY ◯	④	④
JUN ◯	⑤	⑤ ⑤
JUL ◯	⑥	⑥ ⑥
AUG ◯	⑦	⑦ ⑦
SEP ◯	⑧	⑧ ⑧
OCT ◯	⑨	⑨ ⑨
NOV ◯		
DEC ◯		

GRADE

① ② ③ ④ ⑤ ⑥

(Name and answer grid: columns of bubbles A through Z)

Vocabulary

1 Ⓐ Ⓑ Ⓒ Ⓓ   4 Ⓐ Ⓑ Ⓒ Ⓓ   7 Ⓐ Ⓑ Ⓒ Ⓓ   10 Ⓐ Ⓑ Ⓒ Ⓓ   12 Ⓐ Ⓑ Ⓒ Ⓓ   14 Ⓐ Ⓑ Ⓒ Ⓓ
2 Ⓐ Ⓑ Ⓒ Ⓓ   5 Ⓐ Ⓑ Ⓒ Ⓓ   8 Ⓐ Ⓑ Ⓒ Ⓓ   11 Ⓐ Ⓑ Ⓒ Ⓓ   13 Ⓐ Ⓑ Ⓒ Ⓓ   15 Ⓐ Ⓑ Ⓒ Ⓓ
3 Ⓐ Ⓑ Ⓒ Ⓓ   6 Ⓐ Ⓑ Ⓒ Ⓓ   9 Ⓐ Ⓑ Ⓒ Ⓓ

Reading Comprehension

1 Ⓐ Ⓑ Ⓒ Ⓓ   3 Ⓐ Ⓑ Ⓒ Ⓓ   5 Ⓐ Ⓑ Ⓒ Ⓓ   7 Ⓐ Ⓑ Ⓒ Ⓓ   8 Ⓐ Ⓑ Ⓒ Ⓓ   9 Ⓐ Ⓑ Ⓒ Ⓓ
2 Ⓐ Ⓑ Ⓒ Ⓓ   4 Ⓐ Ⓑ Ⓒ Ⓓ   6 Ⓐ Ⓑ Ⓒ Ⓓ

Language Mechanics

1 Ⓐ Ⓑ Ⓒ Ⓓ   4 Ⓐ Ⓑ Ⓒ Ⓓ   6 Ⓐ Ⓑ Ⓒ Ⓓ   8 Ⓐ Ⓑ Ⓒ Ⓓ   10 Ⓐ Ⓑ Ⓒ Ⓓ   12 Ⓐ Ⓑ Ⓒ Ⓓ
2 Ⓐ Ⓑ Ⓒ Ⓓ   5 Ⓐ Ⓑ Ⓒ Ⓓ   7 Ⓐ Ⓑ Ⓒ Ⓓ   9 Ⓐ Ⓑ Ⓒ Ⓓ   11 Ⓐ Ⓑ Ⓒ Ⓓ   13 Ⓐ Ⓑ Ⓒ Ⓓ
3 Ⓐ Ⓑ Ⓒ Ⓓ

Language Expression

1 Ⓐ Ⓑ Ⓒ Ⓓ   4 Ⓐ Ⓑ Ⓒ Ⓓ   7 Ⓐ Ⓑ Ⓒ Ⓓ   9 Ⓐ Ⓑ Ⓒ Ⓓ   11 Ⓐ Ⓑ Ⓒ Ⓓ   13 Ⓐ Ⓑ Ⓒ Ⓓ
2 Ⓐ Ⓑ Ⓒ Ⓓ   5 Ⓐ Ⓑ Ⓒ Ⓓ   8 Ⓐ Ⓑ Ⓒ Ⓓ   10 Ⓐ Ⓑ Ⓒ Ⓓ   12 Ⓐ Ⓑ Ⓒ Ⓓ   14 Ⓐ Ⓑ Ⓒ Ⓓ
3 Ⓐ Ⓑ Ⓒ Ⓓ   6 Ⓐ Ⓑ Ⓒ Ⓓ

Spelling

1 Ⓐ Ⓑ Ⓒ Ⓓ   3 Ⓐ Ⓑ Ⓒ Ⓓ   5 Ⓐ Ⓑ Ⓒ Ⓓ   6 Ⓐ Ⓑ Ⓒ Ⓓ   7 Ⓐ Ⓑ Ⓒ Ⓓ   8 Ⓐ Ⓑ Ⓒ Ⓓ
2 Ⓐ Ⓑ Ⓒ Ⓓ   4 Ⓐ Ⓑ Ⓒ Ⓓ

Math Concepts

1 Ⓐ Ⓑ Ⓒ Ⓓ   4 Ⓐ Ⓑ Ⓒ Ⓓ   7 Ⓐ Ⓑ Ⓒ Ⓓ   10 Ⓐ Ⓑ Ⓒ Ⓓ   13 Ⓐ Ⓑ Ⓒ Ⓓ   16 Ⓐ Ⓑ Ⓒ Ⓓ
2 Ⓐ Ⓑ Ⓒ Ⓓ   5 Ⓐ Ⓑ Ⓒ Ⓓ   8 Ⓐ Ⓑ Ⓒ Ⓓ   11 Ⓐ Ⓑ Ⓒ Ⓓ   14 Ⓐ Ⓑ Ⓒ Ⓓ   17 Ⓐ Ⓑ Ⓒ Ⓓ
3 Ⓐ Ⓑ Ⓒ Ⓓ   6 Ⓐ Ⓑ Ⓒ Ⓓ   9 Ⓐ Ⓑ Ⓒ Ⓓ   12 Ⓐ Ⓑ Ⓒ Ⓓ   15 Ⓐ Ⓑ Ⓒ Ⓓ

Math Computation

1 Ⓐ Ⓑ Ⓒ Ⓓ   3 Ⓐ Ⓑ Ⓒ Ⓓ   5 Ⓐ Ⓑ Ⓒ Ⓓ   7 Ⓐ Ⓑ Ⓒ Ⓓ   9 Ⓐ Ⓑ Ⓒ Ⓓ   11 Ⓐ Ⓑ Ⓒ Ⓓ
2 Ⓐ Ⓑ Ⓒ Ⓓ   4 Ⓐ Ⓑ Ⓒ Ⓓ   6 Ⓐ Ⓑ Ⓒ Ⓓ   8 Ⓐ Ⓑ Ⓒ Ⓓ   10 Ⓐ Ⓑ Ⓒ Ⓓ

Math Applications

1 Ⓐ Ⓑ Ⓒ Ⓓ   4 Ⓐ Ⓑ Ⓒ Ⓓ   7 Ⓐ Ⓑ Ⓒ Ⓓ   10 Ⓐ Ⓑ Ⓒ Ⓓ   13 Ⓐ Ⓑ Ⓒ Ⓓ   15 Ⓐ Ⓑ Ⓒ Ⓓ
2 Ⓐ Ⓑ Ⓒ Ⓓ   5 Ⓐ Ⓑ Ⓒ Ⓓ   8 Ⓐ Ⓑ Ⓒ Ⓓ   11 Ⓐ Ⓑ Ⓒ Ⓓ   14 Ⓐ Ⓑ Ⓒ Ⓓ   16 Ⓐ Ⓑ Ⓒ Ⓓ
3 Ⓐ Ⓑ Ⓒ Ⓓ   6 Ⓐ Ⓑ Ⓒ Ⓓ   9 Ⓐ Ⓑ Ⓒ Ⓓ   12 Ⓐ Ⓑ Ⓒ Ⓓ

VOCABULARY

Directions: Find the word (or words) that mean the same or almost the same as the underlined word.

Examples:

1 A <u>cheerful</u> woman

  A unhappy

  B jolly

  C sorrowful

  D silent

2 A loud <u>chuckle</u>

  A roar

  B growl

  C laugh

  D whimper

Answer:

1 **B** jolly

2 **C** laugh

---

1 <u>reliable</u> car

  A good

  B dependable

  C rusty

  D untrustworthy

2 stared in <u>disbelief</u>

  A understanding

  B amazement

  C happiness

  D not believing

3 to be <u>grumpy</u>

  A angry

  B silly

  C fat

  D sad

4 hold it <u>carefully</u>

  A unexpectedly

  B formally

  C gently

  D urgently

Directions: For questions 5–8, find the word that means the opposite of the underlined word.

Example:

The woman was <u>fortunate</u>

  A sick

  B unlucky

  C pretty

  D peculiar

Answer:

  B unlucky

5   <u>angry</u> tone of voice

   A   colorful

   B   happy

   C   furious

   D   silly

6   <u>elegant</u> restaurant

   A   expensive

   B   beautiful

   C   casual

   D   stuffy

7   <u>iridescent</u> butterfly

   A   shiny

   B   ugly

   C   green

   D   dull

8   <u>absolutely</u> the last time

   A   possibly

   B   definitely

   C   lately

   D   surely

Directions: Choose the single word that correctly completes both sentences. These are words that are spelled the same but have different meanings.

Example:

   We have the _____ to speak. I play cards with my _____ hand.

   A   right

   B   wrong

   C   left

   D   other

Answer:

   A   right

9   What _____ of toothpaste do you use?

   Are you going to _____ the cattle at the ranch?

   A   type

   B   brand

   C   kind

   D   feed

10   We are going to take a trip to the _____.

   If the brakes on my car fail, I will have to _____.

   A   beach

   B   mountains

   C   stop

   D   coast

GO

11 We are going to dress for the

_____.

Let's go play tennis with the new

_____.

A ball

B dance

C racket

D court

Directions: Choose the sentence in which the word <u>tap</u> means the same as in this sentence: Let's turn on the hot water <u>tap</u>.

12 A Don't <u>tap</u> on the window pane.

B I can't reach the kitchen <u>tap</u>.

C <u>Tap</u> her lightly on the head.

D She likes to <u>tap</u> dance.

Choose the sentence in which the word <u>pen</u> means the same as in this sentence: Let's put the animals in the <u>pen</u>.

13 A Did you bring a fountain <u>pen</u>?

B Susie will <u>pen</u> the animals up.

C Kurtis would rather use a pencil than a <u>pen</u>.

D It's time to put the rabbits back in their <u>pen</u>.

Directions: For questions 14 and 15, choose the answer that best defines the underlined part.

Example:

<u>over</u>cooked

A cooked too little

B cooked too much

C cooked just right

D none of the above

Answer:

B cooked too much

---

14 <u>re</u>peat or <u>re</u>read

A less

B do again

C more

D louder

---

15 <u>pre</u>order or <u>pre</u>ordain

A after

B again

C before

D more of

STOP

READING COMPREHENSION

Directions: Read the passages and answer the questions that follow. Choose the answer that seems best.

Every year, cats of all kinds converge on Madison Square Garden in New York City as hundreds of cats compete in the International Cat Show there. More than 20,000 people crowd into the arena to see the cats compete for prizes. Judges examine the purebred animals who compete for recognition as best of breed. Family pets (even cats adopted from shelters!) have their own contest at the show.

To choose a winner, a cat show judge must compare each cat to the official standard for its breed. That means the judge must look carefully all over the animal, checking size, body proportion, facial features and expressions, and health of eyes and coat. Then each cat is awarded points based on the judge's opinion. In the end, judges total their scores and choose the winning cat.

1 What does a judge look for when choosing a winning cat?

  A health of skin and eyes

  B length of claws

  C intelligence

  D type of collar

2 This passage suggests that:

  A It's easy to be a champion cat.

  B It doesn't matter what cats look like.

  C Americans like dogs better than cats.

  D Champion cats must have good breeding, good looks, and good expressions.

3 Cat show owners bring their cats to the show to:

  A Meet other cat owners.

  B Have a nice vacation.

  C Compete for prizes.

  D See who is the best judge.

Long before people ever thought about planting corn and harvesting grain, leafcutter ants were tending their underground gardens. The ants collect bits of leaves, then they bring them to underground chambers where the ants grow a white fuzzy fungus on the grass that they like to eat. This particular type of fungus is found only among leafcutter ant colonies.

Leafcutter ant colonies are very large—as many as 5 million ants live in each one—so they need lots of food. It takes a lot of work to get enough food to go around. Each ant in the colony has a job: Some harvest the fungus, some prepare the leaves, and others protect the colony against attack.

The leafcutter farmers fertilize their fungus by spreading their own body waste on the garden. Ant cutters collect fresh leaves and carry them home, where the chewers squeeze and soften the chopped leaves. Ant pasters add fertilized leaf bits to the garden, pasting them in with saliva and leaf juice. Ant haulers bring some of the fungus from the old chambers into new ones where they plant it in gardens. The fungus spreads as it grows. Harvesters are the smallest ants; they tend to the underground gardens and harvest the fungus for the rest of the colony.

GO

4 Which of these is a fact that is included in the above story?

  A Each ant in the colony has a job.

  B Ant fungus grows in the ground.

  C Leafcutter ants live together in small colonies.

  D Leafcutter queens don't work.

---

5 The information in this article was written to:

  A Inform people about how leafcutter ants live.

  B Get people to stop killing leafcutter ants.

  C Explain why leafcutter ants are a danger to crops.

  D Explain how to grow leafcutter ants in farms.

---

6 The fungus that leafcutter ants love to eat is found:

  A in small African countries

  B throughout the world

  C in certain types of grasses and leaves

  D only in leafcutter colonies

Directions: Read the following story, and then choose the best answer to question 7.

Laura lived with her family on a small Amish farm in Pennsylvania. Her father, who wore a long black beard, tended cows on their dairy farm. Her mother, Rebecca, sewed beautiful quilts and planted large gardens of vegetables in the summer. Her sisters, Sarah and Abigail, shared the job of feeding the chickens and collecting the eggs.

7 What part of the story does this passage describe?

  A the setting

  B the mood

  C the characters

  D the plot

Directions: Choose the correct answer for questions 8 and 9.

Example:

Which of these sentences is an opinion?

  A Chocolate cake is the best kind of dessert.

  B There are 50 states in the United States.

  C Washington, D.C. is the capital of the United States.

  D Whales are mammals.

Answer:

  A Chocolate cake is the best kind of dessert.

---

8 Which of these sentences is NOT an opinion?

  A Jane Smith would make a terrific state senator.

  B The Quark is the fastest car on the market.

  C Mars has two moons.

  D It's harder to ride horseback than to ski down a mountain.

9 Which of these sentences IS an opinion?

A Swiss cheese is a type of cheese with holes.

B The atmosphere above planet earth is a mix of 98 percent oxygen and nitrogen.

C The Lynx is the most comfortable car on the market.

D The Ganges is a sacred river to Hindus.

STOP

LANGUAGE MECHANICS

Directions: Choose the correct punctuation for the following sentences.

Example:

A   "Jill, come here!" cried Mom.

B   Silently, the young boy arrived at home past curfew

C   Im going to buy a cake some gloves and a pair of shoes.

D   What in the world are you doing.

Answer:

A   "Jill, come here!" cried Mom.

---

1   "Are you coming to my house after lunch? Julia asked.

   A   ,

   B   .

   C   "

   D   none

---

2   The cafeteria is open every day for lunch.

   A   ,

   B   "

   C   ?

   D   none

---

3   I don't want to," she cried.

   A   "

   B   ,

   C   .

   D   none

---

4   Susan and Jim went down the street toward the school.

   A   "

   B   ,

   C   !

   D   none

Directions: For questions 5 through 7, choose the phrase that has a punctuation error. If there is no error, choose "none."

5   **A**   We pitched our tent

   B   on the ground underneath, some tall trees.

   C   After that, we unpacked our gear.

   D   None

---

6   **A**   Taking care of rabbits is fun.

   B   John, Susie Q, and Petie

   C   are my rabbit's names.

   D   None

GO ▷

109

7 **A**   Strapping on, my skis

    B   I flew down the mountain.

    C   I love skiing!

    D   None

Directions: For the next four questions, choose the word or words that best fills in the blank with the correct punctuation.

8 _____ I want you to come straight home after school.

    A   No!

    B   No,

    C   "no"

    D   No

9 Our village was settled by a group of Puritans from England on _____.

    A   Sept 3 1799

    B   Sept. 3, 1799

    C   Sept 3, 1799

    D   Sept. 3 1799

10 The single small _____ fleece was as white as snow!

    A   lambs

    B   lambs'

    C   lamb's

    D   lamb

11 We are going to the _____ house for dinner.

    A   Harrises   **B**   Harris'

    C   Harrise's   **D**   Harris

Directions: Choose the answer that shows correct punctuation and capitalization.

Example:

    A   Robert, are you going to the first showing of <u>Pygmalion</u>?

    B   I don't know what the Name of the new Harry Potter book is.

    C   Sharon, our family leaves Tuesday for Paris, france.

    D   Every day of the Week, including Saturday, we go to the gym

Answer:

    A   Robert, are you going to the first showing of <u>Pygmalion</u>?

12 **A**   Sarah and her sister played, in the house.

    B   No, I don't think I want to take that cake to Betty.

    C   I'm not sure, but I think the Station is closed now

    D   are you going to see the teacher today!

13 "I hope that you are going to the _____ Mary said.

    A   park,"

    B   park

    C   park",

    D   park,

STOP

LANGUAGE EXPRESSION

Directions: Choose the best way to write the underlined part of this sentence. If the underlined part is correct, choose "no change."

Example:

The cowboy <u>rode</u> the bucking bronco in the rodeo.

A rided

B road

C were riding

D no change

Answer:

D no change

---

1 The young woman <u>skated</u> brilliantly during the competition yesterday.

A skate

B skating

C were skating

D no change

---

2 Kyle spent all day yesterday <u>cooked</u> in the kitchen.

A cooks

B cook

C cooking

D no change

Directions: Choose the sentence that is complete and correct.

Example:

A Sliding down into the water.

B Crying happily, the girl cradled her new puppy.

C Working all alone at night.

D Up close the window

Answer:

B Crying happily, the girl cradled her new puppy.

---

3 **A** Crawling down the beach.

B The whale followed the ship into the bay.

C Adam and Sam worked hard on their project it was almost finished yesterday.

D Running down the lane goes the dog.

---

4 **A** The fence post fell the storm.

B I like to play in our playhouse at school.

C Runs down the slope of the dune.

D Kellen tried to finish cleaning raking leaves.

Directions: Read this report and use it to complete questions 5 through 8.

1. It can be a lot of fun to <u>work</u> as a reporter on a daily newspaper. **2.** It takes a lot of <u>trainings</u> to become a reporter, however. First, you must graduate from college with a degree in journalism. There are lots of graduates who want to be reporters, so it can be hard to find a job!
3. Most people <u>starting</u> out on a small weekly newspaper to get experience. Reporters work long, hard hours six or seven days a week. You never know when news is going to happen, and you have to be there when it does! **4.** Working on a newspaper can be one of the <u>hardly</u> jobs there is.

5 In sentence 1, <u>work</u> is best written as:

A working

B works

C worked

D as is

---

6 In sentence 2, <u>trainings</u> is best written as:

A training

B trainer

C trained

D as is

---

7 In sentence 3, <u>starting</u> is best written as:

A start

B starts

C started

D as is

---

8 In sentence 4, <u>hardly</u> is best written as:

A hard

B hardest

C harding

D as is

Directions: Read the paragraph below. Find the best topic sentence for this paragraph.

_____. There are many reasons why scientists want to go to the Red Planet: to explore, to learn new things, and to find new minerals. The most exciting reason is to see if there is evidence of past life on Mars. However, the surface of Mars is very harsh and it's not likely that life could survive.

9 **A** Scientists are getting ready to send people to Mars.

B So far only robots have visited Mars.

C Lots of people would be interested in going to Mars.

D There is probably no life on Mars.

GO

Directions: Read the following paragraph and find the sentence that does not belong in the paragraph.

1. At the famous Ice Hotel in Sweden, 125 miles north of the Arctic Circle, visitors can check in and stay overnight in a hotel made entirely of ice and snow.   2. Temperatures inside the hotel stay between 16 and 24 degrees F.   3. Skiing is great fun in Sweden. 4. Every year beginning in October, workers rebuild the Ice Hotel using water from the nearby Torne River. By May, the hotel begins to melt.

10 **A**   sentence 1

B   sentence 2

C   sentence 3

D   sentence 4

Directions: Find the simple subject in the following sentences:

Example:

The <u>beautiful</u> <u>gray</u> <u>horse</u> jumped the <u>fence</u>.
        A   **B** **C**   **D**

Answer:

C   horse

11 The black frisky kitten ran up the tall tree.

A   black

B   frisky

C   kitten

D   tree

12 Trying not to panic, the astronaut pushed the throttle on the spaceship.

A   panic

B   astronaut

C   throttle

D   spaceship

Directions: Find the simple predicate (verb) in the following sentences.

Example:

<u>Andrew</u> <u>leaped</u> into the air, <u>which</u>
  A   **B**   **C**
frightened the <u>rabbits</u>.
               D

Answer:

B   leaped

13 Deanna leaped into the air in an effort to grab the Frisbee.

A   Deanna

B   air

C   leaped

D   Frisbee

14 My grandmother arrived in this country from Ireland many years ago.

A   grandmother

B   from

C   years

D   arrived

SPELLING

Directions: For questions 1–3, choose the word that is spelled correctly.

Example:

The _____ dancer flew across the stage.

A gorgus

B gorgeous

C gorgeus

D gorgeouse

Answer:

B gorgeous

---

1 The _____ light lit up the entire dance floor.

A brilliante

B brilinat

C brilliant

D briliant

---

2 I don't know if the thermometer is _____.

A acurrate

B acurate

C accurat

D accurate

---

3 James turned the most _____ color after eating the bad fig.

A peculier

B pecuilair

C peculiar

D peaculiar

Directions: For questions 4 through 6, choose the word that is NOT spelled correctly.

4 **A** <u>fortunite</u> child

B <u>available</u> chair

C <u>recognize</u> a stranger

D <u>distant</u> planet

---

5 **A** <u>predicted</u> rain

B book <u>author</u>

C <u>originial</u> score

D infectious <u>disease</u>

GO

6 **A**   neat <u>accommodations</u>

    B   tough <u>chalenge</u>

    C   <u>enlist</u> help

    D   <u>rarely</u> helpful

Directions: Find the word that is spelled correctly and best fits in the blank.

7 The wind _____ in the attic eaves.

    A   houled

    B   howled

    C   howlded

    D   howld

Directions: Look at the example of two guide words from a dictionary page and answer the following question:

frill	**front**

Example:

Which word would be found on the page?

    A   frippery

    B   fault

    C   fun

    D   fantasy

Answer:

    A   frippery

---

8 Which word would be found on the page?

    A   fright

    B   friction

    C   frog

    D   froze

STOP

MATH CONCEPTS

Directions: Choose the correct answers for the following problems.

Example:

What number is greater than 10?

A 2

B 9

C 12

D 1

Answer:

C 12

---

1 What whole number is less than 4?

A 7

B 3

C 5

D 6

---

2 Which of these numbers is an odd number and a multiple of 3?

A 9

B 7

C 11

D 6

---

3 Which group of numbers is the expanded numeral for 927?

A 90 + 2 + 7

B 900 + 200 + 7

C 900 + 20 + 70

D 900 + 20 + 7

---

4 What number goes in the box?

225 250 275 300 ☐ 350

A 320

B 375

C 325

D 300

---

5 How would you write 700 + 20 + 3 as one numeral?

A 7,023

B 723

C 7203

D 7230

6 What is the numeral for nine thousands, five hundreds, 3 tens, and 8 ones?

A 953

B 90,538

C 95,308

D 9,538

7 Which of these numbers falls between 34,692 and 36,093?

A 34,789

B 32,693

C 32,691

D 36,094

8 What number is missing from the sequence shown below?

60 56 52 48 40 36 32

A 42

B 44

C 47

D 46

9 Sixty thousand eighty nine =

A 60,890

B 600,089

C 60,089

D 6,089

10 Which numeral has a 6 in the hundreds place?

A 650

B 7,564

C 263

D 156

11 What is 379 rounded to the nearest ten?

A 390

B 350

C 400

D 380

12 The $\square$ stands for what number in $\square \times 12 = 60$?

A 3

B 4

C 5

D 7

13 What number sentence goes with the equation 34 + 2 = 36?

A 36 + 2 = 38

B 36 − 2 = 34

C 34 − 2 = 32

D 34 + 36 = 70

14 Which of these fractions is more than 1/2?

A 1/4

B 2/5

C 3/4

D 1/8

GO

15 Which of these groups of decimals is ordered from least to greatest?

A 5.093   5.129   5.693   5.132

B 6.013   6.134   6.254   6.908

C 4.783   6.904   9.089   2.093

D 2.456   4.509   4.765   3.000

16 Which of these is a group of even numbers?

A 23, 26, 90, 59

B 25, 67, 30, 52

C 12, 24, 46, 80

D 33, 56, 68, 29

17 Maggie bought a sweater worth $18.96 and paid for it with a $20 bill. How much change did she get?

A $1.04

B $7.96

C $8.95

D $6.96

STOP

MATH COMPUTATION

Directions: Choose the correct answer for the following questions.

Example:

$$\begin{array}{r} 5.02 \\ -\ 0.10 \\ \hline \end{array}$$

- **A** 8.42
- **B** 4.92
- **C** 5.92
- **D** 5.12

Answer:

    B 4.92

1
$$\begin{array}{r} 8.78 \\ -\ 0.3 \\ \hline \end{array}$$

- **A** 8.48
- **B** 7.48
- **C** 8.38
- **D** 8.78

2 5008 − 456 =

- **A** 3452
- **B** 4552
- **C** 3522
- **D** 6742

3
$$\begin{array}{r} 407 \\ -\ 43 \\ \hline \end{array}$$

- **A** 264
- **B** 464
- **C** 164
- **D** 364

4 $45.03 − $23.90 =

- **A** 21.13
- **B** 43.13
- **C** 31.13
- **D** 11.13

5 7/11 − 4/11 =

- **A** 6/11
- **B** 11/11
- **C** 3/11
- **D** 2/11

6
$$\begin{array}{r} 9586 \\ -\ 4938 \\ \hline \end{array}$$

- **A** 4538
- **B** 4638
- **C** 4648
- **D** 4628

GO ▷

7
$$\begin{array}{r} 50 \\ \times\ 6 \end{array}$$

A 400

B 30

C 40

D 300

8
$$\begin{array}{r} 40 \\ \times\ 90 \end{array}$$

A 360

B 3600

C 3200

D 320

9 $6 \times 45 =$

A 270

B 260

C 170

D 275

10 $650 \div 5 =$

A 130

B 230

C 430

D 120

11 $6450 \div 5 =$

A 1390

B 1350

C 1290

D 1190

STOP

MATH APPLICATIONS

Directions: Read the following questions and choose the correct answer.

Example:

How many sides does the figure below have?

A   4

B   3

C   2

D   5

Answer:

B   3

---

1   How many sides does this shape have?

A   3

B   4

C   5

D   6

2   What is the area of this shape?

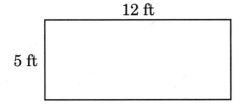

12 ft

5 ft

A   50 ft

B   60 ft

C   120 ft

D   17 ft

3   What is the perimeter of a square room if each side is 12 feet?

A   48

B   24

C   36

D   480

4 Which of the following shapes is a cylinder?

A

B

C

D

5 What are these lines:

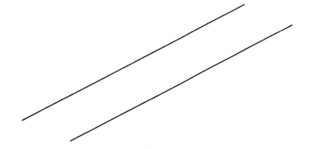

A perpendicular

B intersecting

C parallel

D rays

6 Which one of these figures shows a circle inside a rectangle?

A

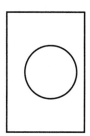

B

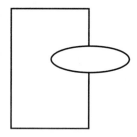

C

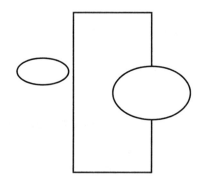

D none of these

GO

7 What is the length of this feather?

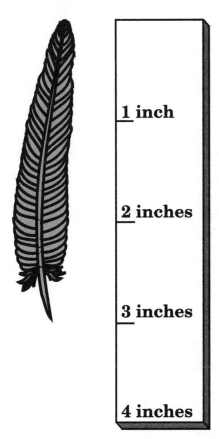

A 1 inch **B** 2 inches

C 3 inches **D** 2 1/2 inches

8 What time is shown on the clock?

A 7:45 **B** 10:20

C 7:50 **D** 7:55

9 If you had one quarter, three dimes, five nickels, and five pennies, which of these could you buy?

A a shirt for $8.50

B a burger for $1.05

C a candy bar for 85 cents

D a soda for 75 cents

10 How many hours are there in three days?

A 24

B 48

C 36

D 72

11 What temperature does this thermometer show?

A 92 degrees **B** 95 degrees

C 90 degrees **D** 5 degrees

12 How would you write 43 cents as part of a dollar?

A 43$

B $.43

C 43.00

D $43.00

13 You want to find the average weight of four dogs. One weighs 10 pounds, one weighs 30 pounds, one weighs 54 pounds, and one weighs 72 pounds. How do you find the average?

A Add all the weights and multiply by four.

B Add all the weights and divide by four.

C Multiply the weights together and divide by four.

D Divide the weights by 4 and then add 5.

14 Susan got up at 5:00 a.m. It took her 30 minutes to get dressed and eat breakfast, and an hour to get to ballet class. Class took 30 minutes, and then Susan spent 15 minutes walking to the restaurant on the corner to meet her mother. What time did she meet her mother?

A 8:15

B 9:15

C 7:15

D 10:15

15 If you hiked three miles every day in April, how many miles had you hiked by the end of the month?

A 84

B 74

C 90

D 184

16 Grace and her family drove two days to get to their vacation home. They spent a week there, and then drove home. How many days were they away in all?

A 10 days

B 9 days

C 11 days

D 7 days

STO

Answer Key for Sample Practice Test

Vocabulary

1	B
2	D
3	A
4	C
5	B
6	C
7	D
8	A
9	B
10	D
11	A
12	B
13	D
14	B
15	C

Reading Comprehension

1	A
2	D
3	C
4	A
5	A
6	D
7	C
8	C
9	C

Language Mechanics

1	C
2	D
3	A
4	D
5	B
6	C
7	A
8	B
9	B
10	C
11	B
12	B
13	A

Language Expression

1	D
2	C
3	B
4	B
5	D
6	A
7	A
8	B
9	A
10	C
11	C
12	B
13	C
14	D

Spelling

1	C
2	D
3	C
4	A
5	C
6	B
7	B
8	C

Math Concepts

1	B
2	A
3	D
4	C
5	B
6	D
7	A
8	B
9	C
10	A
11	D
12	C
13	B
14	C
15	B
16	C
17	A

Math Computation

1	A
2	B
3	D
4	A
5	C
6	C
7	D
8	B
9	A
10	A
11	C

Math Applications

1	D
2	B
3	A
4	C
5	C
6	A
7	C
8	C
9	C
10	D
11	B
12	B
13	B
14	C
15	C
16	C